Heaven and Earth are flowers
Gods as well as Buddhas are flowers
The heart of a human is also the soul of flowers

HEAVEN AND EARTH ARE

flowers

REFLECTIONS
ON IKEBANA
AND BUDDHISM

Joan D. Stamm

WISDOM PUBLICATIONS • BOSTON

WISDOM PUBLICATIONS
199 Elm Street • Somerville, MA 02144
www.wisdompubs.org

Library of Congress
Cataloging-in-Publication Data
Stamm, Joan D.
 Heaven and earth are flowers : reflections on ikebana and Buddhism / Joan D. Stamm.
    p. cm.
 Includes bibliographical references.
 ISBN 0-86171-577-2 (pbk. : alk. paper)
 1. Stamm, Joan D. 2. Spiritual biography--United States. 3. Flowers--Religious aspects--Buddhism. 4. Flower arrangement, Japanese. I. Title.
 BQ988.A66A3 2010
 294.3092--dc22
 [B]

The cover poem is from *Japanese Floral Art: Symbolism, Cult and Practice* by Rachel Carr (1961), D. Van Nostrand Company.

The haiku "in cold water..." by Issa was translated by David G. Lanoue and appears with his permission.

The haiku "my well bucket..." by Chi-yojo is from *Far Beyond the Field* by Makoto Ueda (2003), Columbia University Press.

The poem "A Flower Does Not Talk" by Abbot Zenkei Shibayama appears with permission by Charles E. Tuttle Company.

All other haiku and poetic verse have been translated by R.H. Blyth, *Haiku Volume 1–4*, (1981–82), Hokuseido Press.

Photographs of the author's ikebana arrangements are by Derk Jager.

Portions of "At Daikaku-ji" first appeared as "The Way of Flowers" in *Chrysalis Reader* (1998), *Utne Reader* and *Best Spiritual Writing* (2001), and as "Ikebana" in *Tricycle: The Buddhist Review* (2000).

13 12 11 10 09   5 4 3 2 1

Cover and interior design by Gopa & Ted2, Inc. All photo by Derk Jager.
Set in RialtoDF Piccolo 12/17.

2009044744

Printed in the United States of America.

IN MEMORY OF:

my mother—Faye Irene Stamm
(May 2, 1923–June 1, 2005)

and

my ikebana teacher—Mary Hiroko Shigaya
(February 15, 1925–April 21, 2007)

INORIBANA USING GLADIOLA AND CROCOSMIA.
ORIGINAL CONTAINER BY RON CARSON.

Contents

Prologue

Flowers are tokens of love. Even in our ordinary secular lives we give flowers to those who are sick or troubled, or are graduating, having a birthday, having a baby, getting married. We give flowers to the deceased. Why? Because we love them, and flowers symbolically express our pure love, our feeling of the divine whether we are religious or not. Why else would we carefully examine every pink, red, salmon, white, and multi-colored geranium in order to find a precise and most beautiful color combination, then drive ten miles on a rainy day in May to the cemetery, get out our bucket, trowel, and garden gloves, tromp over to our mother's grave in the wet grass, and plant those cheerful pink geraniums in ceramic containers beside her tombstone? Because she loved geraniums, because every year when she lived in the country she would grow geraniums from starts in round black pots on her patio, winter them in a greenhouse or a garage, water them all through November, December, January, February, March, and April, so she could grow them again in pots on her patio. And she would do this even when she was confined to a wheelchair, except then she picked out geraniums at the nursery; she examined every color combination, usually choosing pink or sometimes salmon, never red or white. Then with our help, because she couldn't push a cart or drive a car or lift boxes of geraniums anymore, she brought her precious geraniums home to her assisted living patio, her 6' x 10' cement slab of heaven that was so jammed with flower pots, planters, starts, slips, and little sprigs of things growing in Styrofoam cups that she barely had room for her wheelchair. There in the midst of her patio squalor, she repotted her geraniums in cedar containers and lamented the fact that she had no place to winter them anymore. Despite her complaints and aching body, she looked forward to entering her outdoor cathedral in the evenings to snip and trim and water in the cool and quiet. She reveled in her oasis of spiritual splendor even though this haven became ever smaller as she grew ever more frail.

My mother's religion of flowers, of bathing in the bliss of living things, gave her a reason to live. She would stay outside among all her favorite annuals and perennials until exhaustion forced her to go inside where ordinary mundane life and domestic duties bound her to earthly sadness.

Given that flowers, plants, and all living things express and give rise to this highest state of human experience, our love and sanctified joy, is it any wonder that we put flowers on altars, and offer flowers to buddhas?

A world of grief and pain:
Flowers bloom,
Even then...

—ISSA

Preface

In the year America began its first bombing campaign in Iraq, 1991, my sister took a teaching job in Kobe, Japan, complete with a three-bedroom house in the countryside. Since I had no personal commitments that kept me bound to life in the U.S., I quit my job, sold my furniture, found a parking space for my truck and a loving home for my cat, and left Seattle to join her. I was thirty-eight.

When I arrived in Japan, I had no job prospects, a credit card debt of six thousand dollars, and enough cash to last about three months. By the end of the year, I had three part-time jobs: two teaching English conversation and one editing books. The editing job brought me into contact with a Shinto organization concerned with the preservation of a two-stringed *koto*, a traditional musical instrument used in religious rituals, and the teachings of Konko

Daijin, a nineteenth-century farmer and realized being who incorporated Buddhism into Konkokyo, a modern form of Japan's native Shinto religion. Konko Daijin believed in the truth of all religions and said, "Open your heart, have a broad mind, and be a person of the world." His philosophy echoed my own, then and now.

In the same year Saddam Hussein's armies invaded Kuwait, 30 million Africans faced famine; 300,000 Somalis lost their lives in that country's civil war; 4.6 million residents of the Horn of Africa languished in refugee status; and a campaign of "ethnic cleansing" in Yugoslavia began to claim the lives of over 100,000 men, women, and children through rape, torture, and mass killings. The Buddha's First Noble Truth, the truth of suffering, glared from the cover of every newspaper and magazine.

Feeling powerless to stop others' suffering, I grappled with the complexity of human tragedy through writing, and later through the study of Buddhism as I began to explore Buddhist temples in and near Kobe, Kyoto, and Nara. My two "pilgrim's books" began to fill with calligraphic stamps, one each from fifty-six temples. But, of course, merely visiting temples and looking at tourist brochures did not satisfy the deeper yearning I had. I wanted to understand the teachings and practices of Buddhism.

The Zen temples often allowed lay people to meditate with them for a few hours, for a day, or even for a week, during *sesshins*, the intensive monastic meditation retreats. I visited temple *zendos* (meditation halls) a few times and soon started meditating every night at home. I would sit on the edge of my futon, place a candle in front of me on the *tatami* mat, and silently observe my breath. To celebrate my fortieth birthday, I dragged my sister to the International Zen Center; the trip from our house took three hours by train, thirty minutes by bus, and twenty minutes by foot. For two days we followed the daily schedule: rising at 4:30, chanting at 5:00, meditating at various times the rest of the day, working for two hours in the afternoon. Even eating is part of Zen training—eat without distraction, eat everything, be purposeful, be silent and clean your bowl with hot water and a pickled radish. My sister nearly gagged when we had to drink the water used to clean our food bowls.

That same year, a Soto Zen priest who presided over our neighborhood temple offered to teach me Zen philosophy, but the Japanese friend that introduced us didn't want the responsibility of providing interpretation, and I wasn't able to find anyone who would. I had to decline the priest's generous offer. Later I would regret that I didn't apply more effort in seeking an interpreter. I liked the monk's kind spirit and generosity. He conveyed loving compassion and an open heart in a way that drew a core of devoted students. He could have been my first authentic spiritual guide. But perhaps I wasn't ready. Even so, the temple experiences I had in Japan ripened my determination to discover more about Buddhism than I could glean from a book. Many of the monks I met exuded a special quality of kindness, serenity, and humility mixed with a disciplined countenance not often found in lay people.

When I returned to the States, I knew I wanted to find a Buddhist teacher. In the years that followed I would explore both Zen and Tibetan traditions as they are taught and practiced in the West. Although I had begun my search for a spiritual discipline, I also yearned for an artistic path that had evolved out of a Japanese Buddhist tradition. With an undergraduate degree in visual art, my training in form, color, line, and texture would naturally take me to the study of *ikebana*, the Japanese art of flower arranging. But these words—"flower arranging"—do not begin to describe the complex system of rules, artistic principles, and symbolic meaning found in this art form. By observing the beauty and quietude of nature; the play of opposites, of *yin* and *yang* (*in* and *yo* in Japanese); and the asymmetrical balance of line, mass, and empty space, the ikebana practitioner strives to incorporate peace, harmony, reverence, and a feeling of centeredness into his or her arrangement and into daily life. The connection with nature, and the pursuit of the spiritual through ikebana, a word that literally means "living flowers," is the greater study of Kado, the Way of Flowers.

With ikebana, the artist does not need a special studio or storage space for practice objects, as with oil paintings, ceramics, or metal sculptures. Flower creations can be born in one's kitchen, die a natural death, and be composted in the garden. The impermanence aspect of ikebana appealed to my poetic sensibility, my sense of life's ephemeral nature.

One night, knowing very little about the history or styles of different ikebana schools, I signed up for a class at the Hyogo Cultural Center in downtown Seattle. The ancient Buddhist temple pictured on the cover of the school's brochure immediately hooked my attention; it looked familiar.

The Saga School of Ikebana maintained its headquarters at Daikaku-ji, a temple compound in the Arashiyama suburb of Kyoto rimmed by mountains, rice fields, and bamboo forests. When I lived in Japan, I had visited this region many times on weekend getaways from my teaching jobs in Kobe. One summer, in the impossible humid heat of August, I took the wrong bus to Arashiyama and ended up wandering down a road amid radish fields trying to find one of the few temples in Kyoto I hadn't yet visited. The high-pitched sound of thousands of cicadas, together with the intense heat, created a dream-like quality that reminded me of the slow, hypnotic movements of actors in a Noh play—the reality of the mundane world blends with that of "other" worlds while the priest intones, "Uncertain the journey's end, our destination uncertain too, the place from whence we come."

I remember passing a young boy and his father walking in the field. They were city people, not farmers, and I suspected that the boy, probably a member of a popular local bug-collecting club, had enlisted his father into helping him snag a prize specimen. I kept on walking, determined to find the temple. A few minutes later, as I stood on the side of the road scrutinizing my map, a car pulled up beside me. The driver asked if I wanted a lift. It was the father and son from the radish field. We were the only three people on the road that day, and if this scene had been in the U.S. I would have felt vulnerable, cautious, and a little scared—not so in Japan. In Japan, I felt perfectly safe accepting a ride from a stranger.

After a few twists and turns down narrow roads, we pulled up to the front gate of a Heian-period temple: Daikaku-ji. The father and son waved goodbye and I stepped out onto the hallowed grounds of the elusive temple. An ikebana exhibition on display along the entrance to the temple turned out to be the new Shinshoka style

SHINSHOKA USING CANNA.

that uses very few flowers to create a dramatic yet simple statement. I particularly recall one lime-green anthurium in a rust clay bowl. I would not know for another twelve years that Shinshoka, developed at Daikaku-ji the previous year, represented a new trend toward an environmental statement for the twenty-first century; nor would I know that one of the styles, Inoribana, or Prayer Flower, would someday be the underlying theme of a book. I also did not know until that night at Hyogo Cultural Center that this great temple housed the international headquarters of the Saga School of Ikebana. Even more serendipitous, this new style that very much appealed to my love of simplicity would become the focus of my completion certificate demonstration when, fourteen years later, Daikaku-ji gave me official permission to teach ikebana.

In retrospect, the path of Kado began to unfold that night at the Cultural Center when I saw the brochure with Daikaku-ji on the cover. Later when I met the head of the school, Mary Hiroko Shigaya, a sweet, welcoming, and knowledgeable Buddhist woman who agreed to be my teacher, I knew I had found something very special.

After my time in Japan, I vowed to find what the Buddhist path calls "right livelihood," and *do something* tangible about human suffering. For the next eight years, I assisted African, Middle Eastern, and Russian refugees in achieving their goal of U.S. citizenship. In my free time I continued to study ikebana and Buddhism. During those eight years, I heard accounts of every brutal war atrocity. I listened to dozens of heartbreaking stories of escape. Many nights after work, completely drained of my life force, I headed into rush hour traffic wiping tears from my eyes as I recalled a client's painful story. Fueled by the unrelenting suffering of refugee life, the incomprehensible brutality that created refugee situations, and my inability to alleviate or change suffering in any significant way, I turned with new vigor to Buddhism for relief and answers. For a while, my job and my Buddhist studies, practices, and retreats took most of my time and energy. I started skipping my ikebana lessons, even though I should have known better.

From an early age, I had learned from my mother what solace can be found in a living plant, a flower. Unable to find much pleasure in ordinary life, she filled her days with hollyhocks and hydrangeas, dahlias and daisies, gladiolas and sweet Williams. She dug up trilliums in the forest and brought them back to her garden, snipped peonies from abandoned farms, snuck coleus slips in her pockets while visiting nurseries and always had geraniums, impatiens, and lobelias on her patio. In the North Dakota winters of my youth, she would spend evenings thumbing through seed catalogues, not because she planned on ordering anything "so expensive," but because she needed the life force of flowers—if only pictures of flowers—to sustain her. She once said that if she couldn't take care of her flowers anymore she might as well be dead.

And so, one day, feeling completely powerless to end human suffering, and feeling the absence of artistic tranquility in my life, I resumed my ikebana studies with Mary.

Despite my job fatigue, I attended classes after work and forced myself to be creative. Each ikebana arrangement became the one joyful, beautiful thing I produced in the midst of endless suffering and sorrow. Flowers became a lifeline back to the highest and simplest part of myself. In one subtle way, through the act of artistic creation, I defied misery, war, killing, and even death. The universal life energy of flowers, of living things, began to renew my spirit.

One day, at the edge of spring and eight months after the death of my mother, I finally saw for myself the Buddha's truth of the reality of suffering, suffering that could never be ended by ordinary, worldly means. I said goodbye to all of my grateful and loving refugee clients, goodbye to endless phone calls, e-mails, immigration meetings, office politics, and stress. I resigned, and left for Japan two weeks later to reconnect with the culture that had profoundly influenced my thinking and my life.

This book touches on the spiritual highlights of my life with ikebana, Buddhism, and Japan, a journey and a circle not yet complete.

Morning cold;
The acolyte intones the sutra
Cheerfully.
—SHIKI

At Daikaku-Ji:

GREAT ENLIGHTENMENT TEMPLE

Surrounded by cherry trees, pagodas, and stone statues of Buddha, Osawa Pond at Daikaku-ji provides a peaceful shoreline where visitors from all over Japan stroll and stare and feed the fat carp swimming beneath its surface. As I walked around the edge, I imagined the phoenix-prowed boats that once sailed these waters and the Heian-era aristocrats who rode them: ladies dressed in twelve shades of silk kimono with hair so long it brushed their toes. Looking across the glassy surface to the vermillion pagoda on the other side, I felt transported to a timeless and unfathomable place.

Daikaku-ji, whose name means "Great Enlightenment Temple," was once the summer palace of Emperor Saga who reigned at the beginning of the Heian Period, a golden era of artistic and cultural achievement lasting three hundred years. According to legend, the emperor was one day sailing on Osawa pond when he picked chrysanthemums from one of the two islands. He returned to his palace and placed the flowers in a vase. In that moment, it is said, due to the pleasing manner of his arrangement, the Saga School of Ikebana was born.

After Emperor Saga passed away, his daughter Empress Seishi converted the Saga Palace into a Shingon temple in honor of her father's great admiration for Kukai, the monk who brought Shingon Buddhism from China to Japan in 806 C.E. Eleven hundred years later, Daikaku-ji, still a prominent historical temple in northwestern Kyoto where radish fields meet pine-forested hills, strives "to unite flowers and religion" through its dedication to Buddhism and the art of ikebana.

At 5:00 A.M. on my first morning at Daikaku-ji, clanging bells rang out over the intercom and a monk's cheerful voice said in Japanese, "Good morning! Today is Monday, October 29!" I pulled the quilt over my head. My mind, doing what it did best (rebelling, thrashing against discipline, rules, and any attempt from the outside to reign in chaos and squelch laziness), had to accept getting up or face the embarrassment of failing before beginning; I'd have to face Maeda-san, the young woman assigned to take me to the forty-minute Shingon sutra chanting. My ikebana studies in the States did not include Shingon Buddhism, but the Saga School in Japan required visitors and resident students to show reverence by attending morning service, a condition that at least one part of me had no quarrel with; I hoped that partaking in a spiritual discipline would deepen my experience of ikebana and myself, even though I did not know what to expect from Shingon other than what one book referred to as "mantra, mudra, and magic."

When Maeda-san and I arrived at the *hondo*, a tour group of twenty middle-aged women had already arrived. They sat together on the opposite side of the room. Maeda-san, five resident students, and I sat on the other side. While we waited, the tour group made a game of batting mosquitoes out of the air. They giggled and took pictures—with a flash. Their actions, so brazen in the inner sanctum of a temple, seemed irreverent even then, years before I would fully appreciate teachings on the karmic dangers of harming sentient beings.

Before the door opened, the students bowed their heads to the mat; the tour group just bowed; I looked up, expectant. The shoji-screen doors slid open and a parade of monks filed into the room.

The monks took their places inside the inner sanctuary, a separate area cordoned off by a low black railing.

Images of Dainichi Nyorai—also known as Mahavairochana Buddha, the embodiment of the all-pervading universal enlightenment—adorned the altar, as did formal flower arrangements called Shogonkas, and glittering gold objects that symbolize the radiance of enlightenment. The priests sat on their heels and arranged long billowy sleeves. The only sound came from the rustle of silk falling in graceful folds. Simultaneously they arrived at correct and poised postures, and then a young monk began the ritual of transporting a sacred text from the altar to the presiding monk. A novitiate began chanting the Heart Sutra, his voice soon joined by the others. The deep melodic sound of male voices, synchronized into rhythmical tones and cadences, heightened my senses, and made me straighten my spine to witness Shingon's "three mystic practices" to achieving enlightenment: sacred body postures, cultivation of faith through meditative concentration, and the divine chanting now reverberating throughout the still morning air.

I tried not to change positions too many times, or in any way act disrespectful, but found that I could not sit on my heels in the proper *seiza* style for more than a minute, and that no one but me was sitting cross-legged. I struggled, in my awkward way, to engage in the third mystic practice—concentration—but drifted off into worries, memories, and questions. Why aren't we chanting with them? How long before they stop? Did anyone see me change my position?

Despite my discomfort, I felt joyful at partaking in a morning religious ritual that had been performed since ancient times. When the service was over and the monks had departed, I held the moment in silence and savored the thrill of it alone; then I filed out behind Maeda-san and retrieved my slippers.

What couldn't be seen earlier in the dark was now illuminated by the bluish light of sunrise—white rock gardens raked into swirling shapes, Japanese black pines trained into long sweeping arches, and dozens and dozens of six-foot-tall chrysanthemums pruned into three-tiered configurations and grouped in patterns of white, yellow, and magenta: the Heaven, Earth, Human principle of ikebana.

Before I could fully absorb the beauty of the temple at dawn, Maeda-san ushered me off to the cafeteria for a breakfast of fish, rice, and an assortment of pickled vegetables. The subtle flavors and delicate textures of Japanese food felt light and healthy. After a lunch of similar fare, I vowed to eat this way during the rest of my stay in Japan, even when I wasn't required to dine at the temple. Eating Japanese food seemed to compliment the discipline of attending morning service and studying flower arranging.

In this mood of aspiration, I began my first ikebana lesson.

Sensei, a thin middle-aged woman with straight shoulder-length hair, wore a fashionable grey knit sweater and skirt and bright red lipstick. Her demeanor, poised and confident, and her face, calm yet animated, reflected the path of balanced living that I sought. Her assistants distributed flowers and vases, and the students took out their textbooks. Since I didn't have a textbook, my translator (Iwata-san, a polished, articulate mother of two who had learned fluent English without leaving Japan) would have to work hard at explaining the techniques and philosophies contained in the books. When Sensei began to outline the prohibitions for choosing and pruning plant material, I realized what a daunting task Iwata-san had taken on. As she translated, I wrote quickly and furiously, scribbling questions and possible interpretations in the margins. Despite Iwata-san's noble efforts, I missed writing down nearly a quarter of the "prohibitions." Among the ones I was able to transcribe were these:

- In traditional arrangements, don't use rice stalks or chestnuts or other plants that are food crops.

- Don't arrange flowers without knowing their names. (*Shows lack of respect for the plant?*)

- Don't use branches that are entangled, as it reminds us of rebellion against one's parents and goes against the teachings of Confucius. (*Rebellion?*)

- Don't use branches that point straight up to heaven; don't use branches that point to earth; and don't use flowers that point to each other. (*Pointing is considered rude? Pointing looks unnatural?*)

- Don't use branches that droop or hang down as they do not look brisk. (*"Brisk"? Was that the right word? Perhaps she meant vigorous.*)

- Don't use branches that are even in height as they will be in conflict with each other. (*One strong line might create a more pleasing design.*)

- Don't use branches that have two outgrowths going in opposite directions. (*Another potential for conflict.*)

- Don't go against the plant's natural growth. (*Follow nature's lead.*)

- Don't have plant materials touching the container.

- Don't make an arrangement that looks like an arrow going toward your guest. (*A suggestion of violence? Disharmony?*)

- Don't use branches that look like the eye of a needle. (*Probably too weird. Unnatural.*)

- Don't use branches that intertwine, look like swords or needles.

- Don't use stems having the same width, instead think of them as strings of a *shamisen*, a Japanese lute. (*Different widths produce a variety of tones, an aura of complexity.*)

- Don't use blossoms that are the same size. (*Not complex enough? Boring?*)

- Flowers should not be hidden or turned away from the viewer. (*Perhaps each flower deserves to be honored.*)

- Avoid placing flowers equidistantly from each other. (*Why did we in the West so relish symmetry?*) Avoid using many different colors, or placing the same color on both the top and bottom of an arrangement.

Sensei went on to say that we must search for the balance of yin and yang, motion and repose, light and dark, active and passive, spiritual and material. She explained the principles of Shinshoka, the new type of flower arrangement for the twenty-first century, which uses fewer flowers to create simple, elegant lines; then she demonstrated one of the Shinshoka styles, Sai no Hana, a modern adaptation of the traditional Seika arrangement.

In a low black bowl Sensei placed an aspidistra leaf at a forty-five degree angle. She placed a dracaena leaf and freesia blossom next to the aspidistra leaf and kept the three stems together so they looked like one. No gaps. Then she de-thorned and pruned a quince branch and showed us how to replace the aspidistra leaf with this new material. Her actions were confident, her movements easy and graceful. Then it was my turn.

Preoccupied by the prohibitions I had not caught, I reluctantly put away my notebook, picked up my aspidistra leaf and stabbed it into the *kenzan*, the needle-pointed plant holder also known in English as a "frog." The leaf drooped off to one side. I straightened the leaf and jammed in the dracaena stem, nearly impaling my forefinger on the kenzan. The dracaena stuck up too high. I readjusted both leaves and put in the freesia. Daylight gleamed through the gaps of the three stems. I pulled them out and tried again, this time using my quince branch.

At the end of an hour I had produced what I thought was a decent arrangement. Sensei smiled and nodded approval, then proceeded to readjust each of my three stems. When she was satisfied with the results she told me to choose a mat to go under my container for display. I chose mint green.

"It matches," she said, and hid her amusement behind her hand.

I quickly replaced the green mat for a dove grey one, thinking grey was a nice, quiet color. But my translator didn't seem to like it.

"Too drab?" I ventured.

"Perhaps."

I only had one other choice: sunflower yellow.

"Yellow?" I said. Everyone smiled with relief that I'd finally gotten it right.

Now I had an arrangement suitable for displaying in the hall with the others. Someone ran off to the office for a name tag and returned with a white card neatly printed with black Japanese characters. The director told me proudly that this was the first time he'd seen a foreigner's name displayed in the school. I knew I wasn't actually the first (only the first he had seen), but the idea pleased me nonetheless. I took a picture to preserve the symbol: transference of culture and spiritual essence.

That night, as I sat on a cushion in my room and contemplated the flower arrangement in the *tokonoma*, the flower-displaying alcove, I felt part of the compositional whole. For one brief moment I became as still and balanced as the flowers. Then, just as suddenly, the feeling vanished and my attention turned to drinking tea and worrying about learning this art form. I fretted over the distance between my current skill and mastery, even though I knew that "mastery" was illusive, that my Japanese-American teacher, who'd been studying ikebana for over fifty years, said she was still learning, still fine-tuning her art. Patience began to factor into the equation; so too did humility.

SAI NO HANA USING ASPIDISTRA, FREESIA, AND HOSTA.

Even so, I obsessed over the prohibitions I'd missed as Sensei was teaching. Was I failing to see the beauty of my own imperfection? My personal asymmetry? Perhaps! But I knew I would ask the teacher tomorrow; I would get all of the prohibitions neatly transcribed in my notebook.

I changed into a *yukata*, a lightweight kimono, and headed for the bath, a public room down two flights of stairs and several dark hallways. Voices, amplified by the acoustics of water, tile, and cement, filtered into the dressing room. Stepping into the steamy bath, I grabbed a plastic pail and sat down beside two of the residents who were already scrubbing and dousing in front of a shower hose. We exchanged polite evening greetings.

As I scrubbed and doused, my mind meandered back to the day's lesson. I remembered that pointing, drooping, entangling, and intertwining are Not Good, that sameness, symmetry, and straightness are Not Good, that something about showing rebellion is Not Good—easy for a plant perhaps, but difficult for an artist who imagined herself resisting the perils of acquiescence, of surrendering to the current.

Completely clean and ready for the bath, I stepped into the stone tub made for five. As my limbs floated in the steaming liquid, the real meaning of *ofuro*, the honorable bath, became completely clear. Like a loyal servant I mentally bowed before its healing vapors, and listened to the sounds of hot water gurgling out of two granite slabs and my own breath, magnified. The prohibitions slipped away, and so too the tensions of being in an unfamiliar place, of trying to understand the finer points of an ancient artistic discipline, of grappling with principles that ran counter to my daily life.

Before my muscles stopped functioning entirely, I rose from the hot water and doused with cold until my body cooled to simmer and my skin began to tingle. Back in my room, I discovered a closet full of futons and, like the princess and the pea, piled them up three high in an effort to simulate a mattress. Content as a centipede in a laundry basket, I fell asleep in the deep silence that resides in a temple at night: calm carried in the scent of burning incense and the counting of breaths by candle flame.

At 4:00 A.M. the buzz of a mosquito made me jump out of bed and flip on the overhead. Once I was up and wide awake and cursing the unnecessary brightness of that light, the mosquito disappeared. How quickly one's harmony could dissolve; how precarious the search for inner peace. All virtues had vanished at the sound of a small insect.

While reviewing my notes, I drank a pot of tea. At 5:20, I scuffled off to the hondo, no longer needing the assistance of Maeda-san. After two nights I had adjusted to the dark and twisting halls, to my slippers scuffling along smooth floors, to young monks darting in and out of sliding doors. My sitting was a little less wiggly and my mind a little less distracted. I thought about the Shingon teaching that we all have buddha nature; that we are all capable of enlightenment. Feeling very ordinary and unenlightened, this view of an inherent spiritual potential appealed to me a great deal. But how to realize my own innate perfection? Vaguely I recalled reading something about artistic creations also being buddhas, that nature, art, and religion are one. This was my starting place and, in the back of my mind, although I kept forgetting, the reason I studied ikebana, the reason I'd felt compelled to journey once again to Japan, and the reason that I would later study and practice Buddhism in earnest.

Before my second lesson, Sensei retrieved the previous day's text so that I could copy the missing prohibitions, and I again added my own interpretations.

- Don't position flowers so that they cover each other. (*Respect each flower.*)
- Don't have two branches going the same direction. (*One cannot follow two paths.*)
- Flowers should not face the viewer like a mirror. (*Narcissism is not good.*)

- Don't have two leaves be directly opposite each other. Prune one or the other. (*Competition creates disharmony.*)
- Don't place flowers as if they are holding each other. (*We should stand on our own, strong and independent.*)
- Avoid black flowers as they symbolize death. (*Don't be morbid. After all, "ikebana" means "living flowers."*)

Having satisfied my compulsion to get all the prohibitions written down, I was ready to learn Morimono, one of five variations of the Bunjinka style. *Bunjin* means "cultured person" and comes from Bunjinga, a Chinese drawing school introduced to Japan in the eighteenth century. The Bunjinka style incorporates freedom of composition and playfulness of design while still maintaining the artistic principles of balance and harmony. Arrangements in this style are given titles taken from either the symbolic meaning of the flowers—pine as eternal youth, rose as everlasting spring—or from old Chinese folk tales and poems.

Sensei instructed us to put the biggest vegetable, a Japanese pumpkin, off to one side, to consider the color combinations, to stack the carrots and peppers and mushrooms in an asymmetrical way, and to remember that groups of three and five are better than four and six, although two is okay. Bitter is good with sweet, green is good with red—again she emphasized the principles of yin and yang, the balance of opposites, the contrasting parts that make a harmonious whole. As I struggled to remember the rules, I lost my own sense of harmony, and in the end, my teacher, ever watchful, always kind and encouraging, had to help me and my arrangement regain balance. Before I placed my Morimono on display, Sensei asked me to name it. "Vegetables Piled Up," I said—a name that appealed to me, even though it lacked the symbolic or poetical reference of traditional Bunjinka.

On my first day off, still strong in my resolve to eat only Japanese food, I headed downtown, fantasizing about lunch at a restaurant I knew. The taste of *nabeyaki* (a kind of vegetable and tofu stew), *donburi* (rice with egg, seaweed, and chicken), and grated radish and cucumber salads beckoned.

My mouth was already watering when I unexpectedly passed a McDonald's. In the States I never ate at McDonald's, but suddenly here in Japan, on my way to eat wholesome Japanese food, I became inexplicably struck with the thought of a Big Mac. A dilemma: two branches, two desires, going in opposite directions. One would have to be pruned. In that moment of weakness when hidden attachments flare up from dark regions of the mind, I turned around and rushed into McDonald's as if a perverse demon had taken control.

In my dazed state of conflicting branches, I found myself saying to the smiling young woman behind the counter, using the almost-English sounding words for a typical hamburger meal "set," "*Bigu Macu Seto, kudasai.*"

"*Drinku?*" she asked.

"*Cora,*" I said.

She filled my tray with a Big Mac, french fries, and a large cola before I had time to ponder my actions. I sat down at a table on the third floor, feeling slightly disoriented. Not only did I have two branches going in opposite directions, they were entangled and smacked of rebellion. Before berating myself too harshly, I remembered another Shingon teaching—all desire has at its root the desire for enlightenment. Even though our suffering comes from not clearly seeing the hidden source of desire, and grasping at other objects instead, I commended myself for the impetus toward awakening no matter how perverse its manifestation. Still, on my way back to Daikaku-ji, I stopped by a market and bought a bag of *mikon* (a kind of Japanese tangerine)—perhaps healthy desires should be cultivated after all. That night, I ate a good temple dinner of tofu and cabbage and an assortment of unrecognizable side dishes. Back in my room I peeled a mikon and contemplated the flower arrangement in my alcove. For that rare and illusive moment, peace returned—the compositional whole incorporated desire and the desire not to desire and the permission to desire—and then, as before, the realization vanished and I reverted to being a pitiful human: alone, apart, separate from the arrangement. I ate another mikon and headed for the ofuro.

The week passed quickly. My last lesson took me back to the religious roots of the Saga school and the "six elements" described in Shingon Buddhism: Earth, Water, Wind, Fire, Space, and Consciousness. Symbolically, these six elements embody aspects of buddha nature, each one perfect unto itself but not existing apart from the whole. I arranged my flowers to personify the six elements, using long sweeping willow branches for Fire and Water, a pruned azalea branch for Wind, leathery ferns for Earth, pink amaryllis for Space, and yellow lilies with cedar for Consciousness. When I ceased fidgeting with my flowers, I saw the achievement of balance and felt the calm of an arrangement well done. The colors created harmony, the six elements worked as a dynamic unit, the whole radiated oneness of body and mind.

On my last morning at Daikaku-ji, a national holiday left me the only lay person in the temple. A young monk gave me permission to explore on my own and take photos; then he scurried off to make his rounds with pots of hot tea and bowls of rice.

In a few hours the temple would open to the public and throngs of tourists from all parts of Japan would come to see the chrysanthemums: national flower and symbol of the imperial family. The sightseers would stand on the veranda over Osawa Pond and take pictures of each other, then tour the grounds before boarding buses back to their hometowns. But at that hour of early dawn, I had the temple to myself.

The centuries-old planks creaked beneath my slippered feet as I moved among giant chrysanthemums—Heaven, Earth, Human; white, yellow, mauve—repeating in patterns at the edge of raked stones. A raven called out from the top of a Japanese black pine and mourning doves cooed under tiled eaves oozing with the smell of sandalwood incense. I associated that smell with peace and calm and reverence and hoped it would permeate my clothes and hair; I yearned to take that scent home.

Stepping out on the veranda, I watched the sun rising over Osawa Pond. Light filtered through orange leaves of split-leaf maple and transformed it into a burning bush. I raised my camera, composed my shot, but did not click the shutter. The radiance of nature would have to live on in my flower arranging—in the yin and yang of ikebana—and in me, during those rare moments of awareness when conflict and rebellion vanished and I melded into the compositional whole.

Something dropped; it is just this.
Nowhere is there any impediment.
Mountains, rivers, and the great earth,
All manifest forth the Body of Buddha.

—ENJU

Rokudai:

THE SIX GREAT ELEMENTS

The slow local train on the Nankai line winds along the steep mountain sides of Mount Koya, making a high-pitched screeching, groaning sound: an other-worldly sound, eerie, but not foreboding. As we climb higher through the Kii mountain range of south central Japan, wisps of fog hang in the valleys and disappear into forests of cryptomeria and bamboo bent with the weight of winter rain. The train enters and exits half a dozen tunnels— dark, light, dark—and each time our eyes adjust and refocus. We move higher and deeper into the mountain, now shrouded in a foggy mist that sweeps up the craggy rocks like silk garments of *tennyo*, female bodhisattvas who fly on clouds and lead beings to the Pure Land.

At the end of the line, now at least ten degrees colder

than the Kansai valley, we transfer to a cable car that pulls us straight up to three thousand feet above sea level where the temperature plummets to nearly freezing. Surrounded by eight peaks, said to represent the petals of a sacred lotus, Koya-san remains the ancient home of Shingon Buddhism, the same esoteric sect found at Daikaku-ji in Kyoto. Kobo Daishi, whose posthumous title means Great Master of the Dharma, founded this ancient monastic city in the ninth century under the name Kukai.

A mandatory stop for pilgrims embarking on the eighty-eight-temple route of Shikoku (the island where Kobo Daishi attained enlightenment), Koya-san maintains a viable community of dedicated Shingon practitioners even today. Seekers, moved by the life and deeds of the sacred Daishi, come to this mountain in the garb of the pilgrim: straw hat and white clothes. The staff they carry symbolizes Kobo Daishi's presence: the bodhisattva who walks side-by-side with those who have faith.

After a ten-year absence from Japan, I am delighted to return to this mysterious mountain top with a deeper knowledge of Buddhism and ikebana. My immersion week at Daikaku-ji years ago turned out to be the beginning of a long relationship with the Way of Flowers and the religion that nourished it.

Disembarking from the cable car, we climb the steep steps out of the station and try to decide which bus will take us into the heart of the temple town. I've coerced my sister into making this overnight excursion. Now, as the rain threatens to turn to snow, I worry that she will regret her decision, despite our mutual desire—since the death of our mother—not to travel alone.

As we stand in the penetrating cold of Japanese winter with our umbrellas shielding us from heavy raindrops, my reason for making this journey feels vague and ill-defined. After all these years I'm still sorting out how art and religion are intertwined and relate to my own practice of Buddhism and ikebana.

Ikebana can be viewed as a decorative art or a symbolic art, one that incorporates Buddhist principles of impermanence and universal harmony into flower forms. It is the latter, ikebana as symbolic art, which has held my interest ever since I discovered the Saga School of Ikebana.

The previous year in Seattle, I'd witnessed Seifu Noguchi, a Kado master from the Saga School of Japan, give a profound demonstration of art as symbol.

Mr. Noguchi, a devoted ikebana artist who has made the traditional eighty-eight-temple pilgrimage route four times in his life, stood on the stage in the church hall, poised and ready to re-create the Buddhist universe in a Shogonka arrangement, a style that I had studied at Daikaku-ji before I understood its deeper meaning. The

Shogonka style symbolically creates the Rokudai, or the Six Great Elements of Earth, Wind, Water, Fire, Space, and Consciousness. These elements in turn represent the body and mind of Buddha Vairochana, the Cosmic Sun Buddha, or the original buddha nature from which all phenomena arise.

My mother was still alive then, and I had wished I could have taken her to see this show, even though she didn't understand why ikebana arrangements weren't judged for prizes. She had, in her healthy days before spells of falling and two strokes took their toll, exhibited dahlias and gladiolas every year at the state fair. She dug, dusted, and stored the bulbs all through winter; then watered and sprayed and groomed her plants all through spring until perfect flowers emerged in summer. She loved winning prizes, even though they were only ribbons that she kept in a drawer. But, despite the lack of competition, I think my mother would have enjoyed seeing the ikebana show. Unfortunately, the restrooms weren't wheelchair accessible and she never knew when she needed one. I hadn't mentioned it to her because I knew she wouldn't be able to attend without a lot of worry.

From squeaky folding chairs, two hundred ikebana enthusiasts prepared to watch the construction of the Six Great Elements, while a video camera zoomed in for close-ups and projected them onto a movie screen overhead. The audience watched the arrangement unfold in symbolic and technical dimensions.

Dressed in a brown and grey silk kimono, Noguchi Sensei exuded the confident dignity of his many years of practice and prominence. His assistants, six women dressed in brightly patterned kimonos and one man in a black business suit, would help him create the eight-foot representation of the Great Elements.

The Japanese delegation began by ceremoniously rolling a patio-sized celadon container to the front of the stage. Various shapes of weathered driftwood wired together at protruding angles had been prepared ahead of time to establish a strong base for the placement of the Six Great Elements.

Mr. Noguchi inserted a bundle of fresh pine, symbol of the eternal, into a bamboo tube at the very top of the arrangement. Pine would represent the first of the Six Great Elements: Space, sometimes interpreted as Heaven, that divine abode above the sky. Space is also interpreted as *emptiness*—the Buddhist teaching that phenomena do not have solid, unchanging essential nature.

Below Space, a magnolia branch with long pink flower buds that jutted upward like flames transformed into Fire, the molten energy that heats our planet, warms our skin, and ripens the seeds of our internal and external crops. Without the fire of our outer and inner sun nothing would grow and bloom, not flowers or trees or spiritual realizations.

Stepping back from the arrangement, Mr. Noguchi examined the lines and clipped an extraneous branch, while his assistants moved in short quick steps across the stage to fetch the next element: Earth.

Represented by Japanese black pine, Earth contributed a balancing element to Space and was meant to convey the physical matter of form and flesh that makes up our bodies and our planet, the grounding force of Mother Earth. Noguchi Sensei inserted a strong-limbed branch, snipped out two clumps of pine needles, and looked satisfied with the results. Earth appeared solid and stable.

I furiously took notes, trying to glean every ounce of meaning from the interpretation. "These leaves that symbolize Earth also show that everyone is helping each other just as the Earth supports all the other elements."

Barberry branches, pruned in a curving, flowing shape, symbolized Water, the fourth Great Element. Mr. Noguchi inserted them into their proper place.

Water could be rivers, streams, oceans, rain: the great natural elements that sustained our world; or water could be our bodily fluids that nourish our precious human lives. And the red berries? A reminder of our blood, the vital liquid that carries nutrients through our physical form by way of internal streams and tributaries. Mr.

Noguchi inserted two Water branches under Fire, twisted the end of one to achieve a precise angle, and turned to his assistant for the fifth element, Wind, represented by the curling tentacles of corkscrew willow.

Wind blew above the Earth. Ethereal and pervasive as air, our breath reaching out into space, the oxygen without which humans and animals, and even plants, could not live; Wind, our life force, flowed under Space and out the back of the arrangement.

"This style of arrangement is for the Buddha and Buddhist altars," said the interpreter.

The master and his assistants united all the elements with pine sprigs and ephemeral strands of blue acrylic fiber, the latest fashionable material in the ikebana world.

Five of the Six Great Elements—Earth, Water, Wind, Fire, and Space—stood ready to receive the last Great Element: Consciousness, sometimes referred to as "Mind," or "Heart."

In *Attaining Enlightenment in This Very Existence*, Kobo Daishi says, "The Six Great Elements are interfused and in a state of eternal harmony. " A Shingon monk I know would demonstrate the idea of "interfused" with a hand gesture, a *mudra*: using all five fingers from his left hand (which symbolize the five universal elements), and the index finger from his right hand (which represents individual consciousness, and the sixth element), he joined both index fingers at the tip to show how the two energy forces of wind and breath merge; then he curled the five fingers around the one to show that the two seemingly separate elements were in fact connected, that all of life was interfused in this manner, that the divine permeated or "touched" everything.

In Seattle, to deepen the meaning of the last Great Element, and to enhance the feeling that we are all in this great struggle of life and liberation together, Sensei requested that ten of the American ikebana members each place a red anthurium into the center of the arrangement. The Japanese delegation would each insert a pink cymbidium orchid. In this way we would contribute our own nature, our individual consciousness, to the whole.

Assembled behind the stage, holding the sixth Great Element, our divine tropical flower, we nervously awaited further instructions in our mission to plant the buddha seed of compassion into the hearts of people and nations.

After the devastation of World War II, the Shingon priests must have been pleased to see the symbol-rich Shogonka style developing at Daikaku-ji, to see Rokudai expressed in flowers. Perhaps the priests felt, in some small way, that a Shogonka arrangement depicting the Six Great Elements would serve to remind us of our true purpose in this world—as Kobo Daishi, and other great bodhisattvas have written—"to realize our true divine nature."

SHOGONKA USING HUCKLEBERRY, LEUCADENDRON, SOLIDAGO, IRIS LEAF, FERN, SPIDER CHRYSANTHEMUM, AND ASPIDISTRA.

Standing in the rain with some idea of "truth seeking" tucked into my own inner layers, I wonder if the side trip to Koya-san will fulfill its promise. Will I be able to absorb a layer of the Rokudai mystery in the place where Kobo Daishi's ideas flourish behind temple doors?

My sister and I follow a group of Japanese tourists onto a waiting bus and find seats amid overnight bags and dripping umbrellas. The woman across the aisle, picking up bits of our conversation about where to get off the bus, hands me a map of the area. I smile and accept the map, look at it, nod, show it to my sister, and pretend that it makes sense. Thirty minutes later, after missing our stop and circling back to the beginning of the route, the driver, grumpy from years of dealing with foreign tourists, drops us at a driveway that leads to an ancient *shukubo*, or temple inn. We are too early to register, but the young monk on reception duty stows our bags and tells us to come back after 3:00 P.M.

From the temple steps, we look out into the grey morning and feel suddenly encouraged. The rain has stopped. Downtown is not far, an easy walk. After an hour of obligatory shopping in tourist stores that sell *malas* (Buddhist rosaries) and ritual items relating to Kobo Daishi, we stop for a hot lunch to warm up before making our way to Okunoin, the largest necropolis in all of Japan.

Steam rises from pots of boiling noodles, while marinated beef and chicken crackle on the grill. The kerosene heater is switched off, undoubtedly because the cook is hot. We keep our coats on and warm our hands around a cup of green tea. While we wait for our lunch, I read aloud a passage from the travel brochure: "Kobo Daishi started his eternal meditation in the cave of Okunoin on March 21, 835, at the age of sixty-two and has been believed to materialize his subtle body to the followers." We exchange quizzical looks as if to say, well, maybe.

I think of the "enjoyment body," or *sambhogakaya* in Sanskrit, the body of a buddha only perceived by highly realized beings. Is this the "subtle body" referred to in the passage? Since we will probably not see this body, will we be able to "feel" it among the giant cedars? Will we sense Kobo Daishi's presence emanating from statues of Kannon, the bodhisattva of mercy, or from the dozens of Jizos, statues of the bodhisattva who protect children, women, and travelers.

Energized by our noon lunch, we set out into the cold for the famous cemetery. Along the way we pass a studio with slabs of granite ready to be carved into Rokudai *stupas*. The finished products displayed in front, polished and ready for the engraver, remind me of our mother's gravestone, a polished chunk of Dakota mahogany granite with roses entwined around a cross and two angels trumpeting toward heaven with the words by Ernest Sands: "May the choirs of angels come to greet you."

We cross the Tama River over a white bridge and enter the inner sanctum. Ashes of half a million emperors, lords, samurai, poets, saints, and common people lay entombed under brilliant green moss and towering cedar trees. Eihei Dogen, the founder of Soto Zen, is buried here, along with other great Buddhist masters of past centuries.

We continue down the granite pathway surrounded by thousands upon thousands of stone stupas, some freshly made, others covered with layers of moss and lichen, still others eroding under the weight of centuries, and each one chiseled into the symbols of the Great Elements. The base, a solid granite square, represents Earth. Above Earth, a polished sphere signifies Water. Fire, in the shape of a triangle, points upward to Wind: a half moon that supports Space. Space is shaped like an *ushnisha*, the crown protrusion on Buddha's head that symbolizes enlightenment. The monuments, all in different sizes, represent the unique manifestation of the individual. They radiate out in endless rows and alleyways and spread like a labyrinth of sacred mystery toward Kobo Daishi's tomb. A feeling for the truth that the Rokudai symbols evoke begins to permeate the landscape, making everything appear dream-like, ephemeral: particles moving at a dense rate yet interconnected. My sister and I are moving down the path. We are two characters in a dreamscape. Was our mother's death part of our collective dream? A projection of our own mind? According to certain theories of quantum physics, everything is vibration, thus proving that what we perceive as solid is a deceptive appearance. In the gray light of winter and with the fuzzy tufts of moss blurring the hard edges of granite, even the stupas appear to lack solidity.

As we stroll through the maze of tombs, absorbed in our own quiet moment of awe and reverence, I photograph stupas from the front, side, and back; stupas framed by giant cedars and arching *torii*, Shinto gates leading to spiritual spaces. Only a few other visitors are foolish enough to visit on what locals are calling an unusually cold day. Two women and a girl arrange incense, chrysanthemums, and candles on a family grave; a workman in indigo pants and jacket sweeps cryptomeria leaves from a path; a pilgrim in white with a round straw hat walks along aided by his staff.

By the time we reach the famous mausoleum and the temple of ten thousand brass lanterns, the rain has started again, and a bone-chilling wind begins to blow around the corners of the tombs. We circle the temple perimeter and stop briefly at the gate that marks the entrance to Kobo Daishi's cave. A young woman stands in the shadows praying and quietly crying. We continue on, driven by the cold, the austerity; we are caught in an atmosphere of thick incense smoke, the sound of distant chanting, a bell ringing in some interior place.

With our hands and feet aching from the cold, we are ready for a cup of tea and a homemade sweet at the tea shop in town, but not before lighting our own two sticks of incense, one for wisdom and one for compassion, and requesting that Kobo Daishi walk with us, walk with our mother, walk with all who need comfort.

That night at 6:00 P.M. sharp, a faint rap on our bedroom door signals that dinner is about to be served in an undisclosed location. A shy young monk motions for us to follow him. Stepping into our plastic slippers, we scuffle down a set of steep stairs and cross a wooden veranda that runs along the full length of an impeccably groomed Zen-style garden. The monk stops in front of a set of sliding doors. He opens them to reveal a warmly lit and heated tatami room decorated with painted scenes of stylized Japanese pines. In each of the four corners of the room stand a double set of red lacquer serving tables embellished with an assortment of shojin-ryori: vegetarian food prepared under spiritual discipline, or as The Daily Yomiuri, an English-language newspaper described, food prepared with "zeal in progressing along the path to salvation." The display is strikingly beautiful.

Various forms of tofu, some mixed with pulverized sesame seeds, some cubed and floating in miso soup, or mixed into a thick sweet sauce, complement pickled vegetables, sea greens, kelp, pickled plums, mushrooms (both big and tiny), bamboo shoots, vegetable tempura, baby eggplants small enough to tweezer with chopsticks, steaming rice, a pot of vegetable stew simmering over a burning candle, a tangerine with a sprig of cedar sticking out of an impeccably sliced lid-like top, and of course green tea.

All of the Six Great Elements can be traced in the growing, ripening, harvesting, and making of this food, including Great Heart: the happy minds of the monk chefs who spend all day preparing sauces, slicing vegetables, peeling fruit, and cutting things like lotus roots into shapes of cherry blossoms, a sacred symbol of Japanese spring.

I am reminded of Mr. Noguchi's words when creating the Six Great Elements of his flower arrangement: "Make the Shogonka arrangement with a feeling of gratitude." We eat with gratitude, gratitude for the monks who labored all day to prepare this exquisite meal, gratitude for the beauty of the temple and pristine mountain, gratitude for the opportunity to visit and experience this unique and holy place, and gratitude for the life force that manifests in our bodies and universe.

The following morning, we leave the temple compound in the middle of a downpour, board the bus, the cable car, the train, and ride in silence down the sacred slopes of Mount Koya. The foggy mist still swirls around the rocky crags, and tennyo continue to escort the deceased to the Pure Land, like choirs of angels coming to greet us.

Shortly after our trip to Japan, it is my turn to arrange flowers for our temple shrine in Seattle. I do a simple arrangement consisting of a chartreuse frond from a bird's nest fern, two lavender gladiolas, and three supporting sprigs of Mexican orange and spirea cuttings: an elegant modern arrangement in the Shinshoka style, meant to conserve on plant material by using fewer flowers in bold statements. This arrangement, adopted from the original Shogonka style of the Six Great Elements, expresses the Rokudai principle in the aspect of Inoribana, or Prayer Flower, an arrangement meant to convey simple gratitude.

The leathery fern frond represents Space, and the gladiolas Consciousness: Great Wisdom and Universal Compassion, the yin/yang equation of all existence taught by Buddha Shakyamuni twenty-five hundred years ago. The gladiolas make me think of my mother's garden, the one in the country, and later, the one in town, the patio garden that she struggled to tend right up to her undetected pneumonia. She always planted gladiolas, every year, in every color. Year after year they took blue ribbons at the Fair.

The following day, our resident teacher and head monk presents a day course on the nature of the mind. He says that the mind is like space, like blue sky; it has tremendous power to perceive, to understand, to remember. He points to his heart and says, "All the treasures you seek you'll find in your own mind... this is where your home is. Feel like you are going home."

I think of lavender gladiola, of red anthurium, and pink cymbidium orchid, and I feel the center of my heart opening.

The temple bell dies away.
The scent of flowers in the evening
Is still tolling the bell.

—BASHO

Flower Offerings

To contemplate a flower, a natural mandala of vibrant color and perfect form, is to glimpse the face of the divine. The perfect symmetry of, say, a 'Ramona' clematis with its large pale-blue flowers that open as a six-petaled star, evokes the sacred. And what mystery lies at the center of a purple gloxinia, whose lacy edges encircle velveteen violet petals that deepen from white at the base to purple at the tips as if a light glowed at the center, whose stamens, translucent strands curved and joined at the tip like tentacles of a jelly fish, beckon to come closer, come in.

Flowers, like the various buddhas throughout the world, have aspects, or personalities; they emanate individual characteristics. Take 'Bodacious' for example, a "dinner plate dahlia" whose size and flaming-red boldness smacks you in the face with sheer audacity like the valiance of a dharma protector. Or Japanese wisteria: its weeping clusters of pale blue-violet flowers hang in a bow of deep humility like the quiet nature of Jizo. Whether bold or delicate, bright, bawdy, or barely there, the point is to become absorbed into the deep essence of the flower, to feel its energy and pulse, to forget the self, to gaze into the heart of a living thing and lose your sense of "I."

It's a Friday morning, the day they change the flower offerings at the Seattle Betsuin Buddhist Temple, a Pure Land sangha my ikebana teacher has been a part of for nearly fifty years. The front door is locked but the sign says to ring the bell. A friendly Japanese-American man opens the door and escorts me down several corridors until we reach an alcove where Makiko, the flower-arranger for that week, is absorbed in placing chrysanthemums in a bronze container for Amida Buddha. She has cut a sizeable piece of 'Plum Passion' nandina from the temple garden and placed it center stage in the container; it towers above white, yellow, and mauve chrysanthemums.

Like the man on reception, Makiko is friendly and welcoming. She is happy to discuss flower offerings with me, and says that her arrangements do not follow a prescribed

OMOIBANA USING 'STARGAZER' LILY.

style, that she has freedom to be creative. She is trained in the Ohara School of Ikebana, a style of flower arranging that celebrates natural scenery and colorful Western flowers. The school, developed in the nineteenth century by Unshin Ohara, now has chapters worldwide.

The Ohara School is not the only institution to hold chrysanthemums in high regard—the Imperial Palace adopted the sixteen-petaled chrysanthemum as its royal crest; the Saga School of Ikebana, due to its close connection with Daikaku-ji and the lineage of royal family going back to Emperor Saga, shares it. Thought to have been introduced to Japan from China in the fifth or sixth century, chrysanthemum images are found everywhere in both ancient and modern Japanese textiles, ceramic designs, and poetry.

> White chrysanthemums!
> Where is there a color
> So happy, so gracious?
> —*Yosa Buson*

Perhaps the color itself, radiating from such an exquisite symmetrical form, is lovely enough for the chrysanthemum to be held in such high esteem, though the flowers often appear in poetry and design as symbolic representations. White varieties of this venerable flower denote Heaven, for instance, while yellow varieties signify Earth.

> White chrysanthemums,
> Yellow chrysanthemums...
> Would there were no other names!
> —Hattori Ransetsu

A lush long-lasting flower that blooms in fall, the chrysanthemum sometimes also represents longevity and the culmination of inner riches found after a long life of dedication and devotion.

> They spoke no word,
> The host, the guest,
> And the white chrysanthemum.
> —Oshima Ryota

According to the founding story of Zen, the Buddha held up a single flower, and the disciple Mahakashyapa smiled knowingly. In that moment, the Buddha acknowledged that the true Dharma had been transmitted. Perhaps Mahakashyapa saw that there are no other "names" between heaven and earth, no concepts or analytical thoughts, that our human mind or heart is no different from the buddha nature of a flower. The flower exists as it is in the present moment, full and complete, naked and unfathomable.

In today's Western world, traditions have been supplemented and sometimes replaced by individual creativity. Flowers other than chrysanthemums appear on Buddhist shrines. Makiko says she often uses lilies, or whatever beautiful flowers are growing in her garden. She says this while inserting a few choice purple rhododendron blooms, the Washington state flower and favorite of Northwest gardens. Stepping back, she looks pleased with her finished offering. Together we carry the heavy four-foot-tall arrangement down the corridor and into the worship hall, where the familiar smell of temple incense permeates the air and creates a comforting feeling of "home."

Makiko returns to her alcove while I wander around the temple to view arrangements in other places of worship. Yellow, white, and mauve chrysanthemums predominate, but rhododendron, pine, and cedar can also be found paying homage to images of Buddha. Flower petals, now faded and brown, some already fallen and lying spent on the offering table, show us completion: the cycle of birth, aging, and death, the continual cycle of suffering from which Buddhists seek liberation. Each week, as we buy the freshest flowers for shrine offerings and collect the old, faded, wilted, and brown ones at the end of the week, we are reminded how short life is, how time changes us, ages us, and will eventually claim us.

When I return to the flower alcove, Makiko has placed Japanese maple into two small flower containers. Knowing that maple often wilts when cut, I ask how she will preserve its freshness.

"Saké," she says. "It is drunk on saké. After you cut, dip the ends into saké for a few minutes." She finishes by placing purple and white chrysanthemums into the vase with the "drunken" maple.

Another Friday, and it is my turn to offer flowers to the Buddha. I head to the flower market to see what inspires for this week's ikebana arrangements. I will offer flowers to Buddha Shakyamuni, Tara, Avalokiteshvara, and all the other buddhas, bodhisattavas, Dharma protectors, and lineage holders of our Buddhist tradition while remembering that holy beings are not the true recipients of our offerings. Buddhas, already full of love and light and joy, do not need our gifts of flowers to be happy.

Why then do we take such care with them?

We offer flowers to express our gratitude, but also to practice generosity, to steep our minds in the act of letting go, of giving to others. We offer to make our own minds pure, as pure as the 'Sheer Bliss' rose, its delicate petals a mere blush of color; or the silvery pink Japanese anemone, so fine as to be nearly ethereal. We offer to create favorable causes for ourselves and others, to create a peaceful and pleasant atmosphere so that our minds will become calm. We offer flowers to accumulate positive energy or merit: the favorable karma we need to propel our darkened deluded minds toward higher states, to enlightenment.

In our devotional prayers we sing, "Beautiful flowers, petals, and garlands finely arranged, covering the ground and filling the sky..." and imagine countless offering goddesses emerging out of the love at our heart. They carry single flowers, flower garlands, or flower petals that are then offered to the holy beings. Afterward we reabsorb the goddesses back into our heart. This ritual creates positive karmic imprints in our mind, and beautiful feelings of love and generosity; these in turn help us to experience everything as pleasant. With a pleasant feeling at our heart we no longer attach to anger or hatred, but instead move toward love and compassion. We can then go one step further and transform our kind or virtuous actions into flowers and mentally offer them to the buddhas.

It is April in Kyoto, when cherry blossoms, the national flower of Japan, burst into pink clouds of glory. Saga School ikebana practitioners from all corners of Japan

MORIBANA USING AZALEA AND LILY.

gather at Daikaku-ji to participate in the annual Kenka Shiki, or Flower Offering Ceremony, a three-day celebration honoring Emperor Saga's birthday and requesting purification from Vajra Flower Bodhisattva for having shortened the life of so many living plants. As if to show that the Flower Deity had already accepted the gratitude of the participants, showers of pink petals rain down from cherry trees, anointing heads and robes and pathways with blessings.

Dressed in Shinto-inspired costumes traditionally worn by *miko* (originally female virgins who assisted priests in prayer services), young women in red *hakama* (skirt-like pants) and white silk kimono jackets emblazoned with black designs of paulownia and chrysanthemum assemble in two rows along the temple wall. Each one carries a simple Seika arrangement: a three-tiered configuration of Heaven, Earth, and Human. The flower varieties and colors have been carefully chosen and allocated so that no two women carry the exact same color or flower combination. Yellow buttercups, blue delphinium, white freesia, purple iris, golden orchids, salmon gerbera daisies, lavender balloon flowers, lilac campanula, pink carnations, rose-colored peony buds... all arranged in the Seika slanted style inside aged bamboo containers. The women pull their long white kimono sleeves over their hands—so as not to sully any part of the bamboo container—before they pick up the arrangement and prepare for the blessing ritual.

A young monk in a black robe and white under-kimono strikes a small ritual bell that signals the procession to follow him. He leads the assembly of school officials, professors, monks, teachers, young ikebana graduates, and former headmasters through the meandering wooden corridors of Daikaku-ji to the inner sanctum of the temple. Here, the head monk, a brilliant contrast in his orange robes emblazoned with the white stylized chrysanthemum crest, begins a deep chant while two-by-two the women in red and white walk to the center of the meditation hall, place their flower offering on a table and bow. The ding of a bell punctuates the placing of each offering. After all the colorful arrangements have been lined up two abreast on the offering table, two female professors wearing black kimonos and white masks over their mouths—to avoid contaminating an offering to Buddha—create Seika arrangements to present to Mahavairochana, the Universal Buddha. When finished, they ceremoniously transport the arrangements down a red carpet strewn with flower petals and hand them over to two monks who place the completed Seikas in the inner sanctuary where lay people are not allowed.

After sweets and green tea have also been offered, the monks begin a sacred chant while the head monk performs a blessing ritual. After several congratulatory speeches and promises for the upcoming year, the procession moves out of the temple, past the front gates and over a bridge where the stream below has been christened with layers of falling cherry blossoms. Two male head teachers, wearing elaborate costumes of purple and brown with black hats adorned with flowers, create two more Seika arrangements and offer them at the shrine where copies of the Heart Sutra, transcribed by emperors in times of crisis, are stored.

The monks and all the participants recite the Heart Sutra and then proceed down a gravel path led by the young monk who strikes the bell every few seconds to create the solemn rhythm of their procession. The kimono-clad entourage, mixed with the colorful robes of the monks, ceremoniously walks along the perimeter of Osawa Pond led by the head monk, who strides with a youthful step despite his advanced years. A young monk in black robes shields his master from the sun with a five-foot-diameter red lacquer umbrella.

At last the parade ends at Hana-Kuyo-To, a bronze pagoda built to honor Vajra Flower Bodhisattva, one of many bodhisattvas portrayed in the Diamond Mandala of Shingon Buddhism. The women place their twice-blessed flowers on an outdoor offering table in front of the pagoda. Two more Seikas, this time of cherry blossoms, are arranged by two head teachers and ceremoniously offered.

Again the monks lead a chant of the Heart Sutra, the "Essence of Wisdom" or "Great Mother" teaching. The Heart Sutra, delivered by Buddha Shakyamuni through the Bodhisattva Avalokiteshvara tells us that "form is empty and emptiness is form."

When we offer flowers, we try to remember "emptiness," that there is no "self" making the offering, no ego looking for praise or diminished by criticism, no buddha who receives the offering, no flowers existing in the solid way that they appear. Only the dreamscape, the illusory nature of our world appearing in its many forms, arising, receding, dissolving, arising.... We try to remember that all of life is like a dream appearing to our waking mind, that appearances are deceptive, moments pass quickly, living things are fleeting.

"Beautiful flowers, petals, and garlands finely arranged, covering the ground and filling the sky...." I offer all-white flowers in keeping with the atmosphere of the upcoming course on purification, or eliminating negative karma. I offer calla lilies, king and daisy chrysanthemums with greens of laurel and euonymus, and sprays of variegated sweet flag. In my imagination I offer 'Casablanca' lilies, creamy orchids, stars-of-Bethlehem, white peonies, and all the flowers that are either too expensive, too short-lived, too allergy-producing, or just too unavailable.

In my daily practice, I mentally offer all the orchids at the Seattle Volunteer Park Conservatory; the arrangements at the eightieth ikebana show on Shikoku; the fields of tulips, daffodils, and iris in the Skagit Valley; a dahlia farm I once visited; the Antique Rose Farm; Swanson's and Molbak's nurseries; the wild flowers growing in meadows on the slopes of Mount Rainier that bloom only in August... the possibilities are endless.

My mind mixes with the beauty of flowers, their essence, their celestial faces, as I enter the cathedral of living things, participating as best I can in my own and my mother's religion simultaneously. I am the Human between the white and yellow chrysanthemums of Heaven and Earth.

Heaven and Earth and Human
appear to be different,
but they are essentially one.
This essence has no size,
and the spirit of a human
and the infinite must be one.
—TOJU NAKAE

Heaven, Earth, and Human

The art of ikebana began in the sixth century as flower offerings to Buddha. The arrangements, created in the contemplative environment of the temple compound, expressed reverence for nature, a peaceful heart, and religious devotion. Only monks practiced this sacred art; often, under their vow of "do no harm," they would collect branches that had fallen from trees rather than pick living material. The monks' daily meditation practice brought a humble feeling into their flower arrangements and enhanced their contemplation of impermanence as they observed the seasonal changes, the continuous cycle of birth and death.

Today at Daikaku-ji, ikebana practitioners still study within the hallowed atmosphere of a Buddhist temple compound and attend 5:00 A.M. chanting services with monks; they are still encouraged to contemplate Buddhist sutras before arranging flowers, as evidenced by classes of fifty to eighty students reciting the Heart Sutra before beginning the day's ikebana lesson. A monk from the temple welcomes the students and imparts a short Dharma talk before turning the classroom over to the ikebana professor.

Where I live we do not have authentic Japanese temples. Ikebana studies take place in teachers' homes or shared spaces that offer low rent. Our connection with Buddhism comes in the form of making offerings on shrines—most often in converted Christian churches—or creating a display at the Asian Art Museum where, once a week, members of Ikebana International place an arrangement amid collections of ancient Buddhist iconography from China, Thailand, Indonesia, Vietnam, and Japan. For ikebana artists in the area, this treasure house of gilded buddhas, mandalas, guardian deities, and ritual implements becomes not only the showcase for our weekly flower arrangement, but at least one place where we can reflect on the connection between ikebana and Buddhism.

In July, it is my week to contribute an arrangement to the museum. The evening before, I work out a Moribana style—a modern ikebana in a low black *suiban* container—with the traditional Heaven, Earth, and Human configuration. Originally a Confucian philosophy, the sacred trinity of Heaven, Earth, and Human migrated to Japan from China in the same way as Shingon Buddhism and ikebana. Scholars and translators cannot agree on the original meaning of Heaven, but consensus points to "the Supreme Ultimate," "One," "the Way," and "Nature" as possibilities, not to mention "Heart/Mind" as the place where Heaven resides. It is likely that Heaven is a compilation of all of these elements, which renders it a term that could easily be incorporated into the Buddhist philosophy of Ultimate Truth and the continually residing mind. In this context it is easy to see why the Buddhist priest Gomy adopted the ideas of Heaven, Earth, and Human as one of the main principles for arranging flowers for Buddhist shrines. Along with this original idea of three elements came the philosophy of opposites, or yin and yang; the five elements of wood, fire, earth, metal, and water that permeate and move through the earth.

Heaven, Earth, and Human symbolically form a triangular shape within a square; Heaven is considered to be round and Earth to be square with each point representing the four cardinal points of north, south, east, and west. Heaven, the tallest element or branch, contrasts with Earth, the lowest; Human, the element in between, is represented in Moribana by flowers, but in the traditional style of Seika as merely the middle element.

Heaven, often equated with the male principle, and Earth, with the female, together express a divine union that gives birth to Human. In the yin-yang philosophy, opposites—light and dark, active and inactive, tall and short, empty and full—are the aesthetic principles that ikebana practitioners use to create harmony and balance within the arrangement.

In my Moribana arrangement I use viburnum branches for Heaven and Earth, three red-orange Asiatic lilies for Human, and 'Emerald 'n Gold' euonymus to support the overall design and cover the metal rings of the needle-flower holder (shippo-kenzan). The round, shiny-black ceramic suiban provides a spherical shape for the interior triangle. The empty space opposite the plant material reflects appearances in the expanse of water. The water, filled to the brim in summer, gives a feeling of coolness to the "hot" quality of the orange flowers and the temperature outside.

The following morning, I perform my daily ritual of offering pure fresh water on my shrine, refreshing the begonia blossoms floating in an offering bowl, and lighting a candle and stick of incense before meditating. Then I load my pushcart with bucket, flowers, container, rocks, clippers, towels, and miscellaneous ikebana equipment and drive across town to the museum. By the time I've wrestled my cart up the stairs to the service entrance, I'm usually wondering why I volunteer for this job. Later, after I've absorbed the richness of the environment and received blessings from all of the buddhas, I wonder why I don't do this more often.

At 10:00 A.M. on a Tuesday I am nearly alone in the museum. Only a couple of energetic tourists roam the quiet rooms. As I set out my container, clippers, and drop cloth in the "Asian Aesthetics" room and proceed to recreate the arrangement I worked out at home, a woman spies my activity and says, "Are you the ikebana mobile unit?" I like the image this conjures: solitary artist driving around the city depositing works of flower art in quiet serene places for people's enjoyment and contemplation. What a lovely job that would be! The woman turns out to be a budding ikebana artist from the East Coast who yearns for a teacher in the small town where she lives. I suddenly feel lucky to be living in a place where ikebana teachers from many schools abound, a blessing I've taken for granted.

We chat for a while about various schools and their styles, about modern versus traditional, and then she goes off to the "Sublime and Earthly Splendor" room with Tara, Vajravarahi, Eleven-Headed Avalokiteshvara, and the Thirty-three Deity Vajradhatu mandala from the esoteric practices of Tibet. Left on my own again, I adjust the lilies, directing them toward Heaven while still maintaining the proper line and balance.

Collecting my implements and tidying the display area, I stand back to view my ikebana from a distance. I'm never one-hundred-percent pleased, but nonetheless I call it complete and go off with my cart.

I wander into the "Sacred Rites of Buddhism" room where I am met by an Amida Buddha holding his hands in the teaching mudra. On either side of Amida Buddha stand two bodhisattvas and four guardian kings. The side panel says, "artists were empowered to create the most remarkable Buddhist art as visual representations of the desire to seek sublime beauty and attain enlightenment." Do we still create art with the desire to attain enlightenment? Or have we devolved into creating art for its own sake, or only to provide decoration in a room? A flying attendant, an *aspara*, swoops in on a cloud. He comes from celestial regions in the Buddhist universe that are higher than the human realm but are still within the six stages of *samsara*—the cyclic world of suffering from which we strive to be released.

Before I leave the museum I ask about the "The Descent of Amitabha and Twenty-five Bodhisattvas," a fourteenth-century Japanese painting depicting Amitabha Buddha (one Sanskrit name for Amida) descending from his Pure

Land in the west with a squadron of bodhisattvas all emanating golden light. I am told that, due to a special Chinese exhibit, this famous painting is in storage. What a
shame! The twenty-five bodhisattvas ride on clouds and
move in a descending wave toward a newly deceased person. They play musical instruments, dance, and carry
offerings with the intent of transporting the fortunate
believer in Avalokiteshvara's lotus pedestal back to the
Pure Land. This painting in gold inspires and comforts
the imagination in ways that stone statues in their inert
poses cannot. Death, as depicted in this painting, is not a
black void or existential nothingness, but a beautiful
ascent to golden realms.

As a child I grew up believing in a similar place, a physical place of beauty and light and happy feelings where
"good" people went after they died. Instead of bodhisattvas wearing gold garments, I pictured angels wearing
gauzy blue and white. As a teenager, I would reject the idea
of heaven as a fairy tale, only to discover in adulthood that
perhaps heaven had a deeper, more complex meaning
worth exploring. Through my Buddhist studies I came to
see heaven as an extraordinary state of mind that can be
cultivated here on earth. I came to see that the special quality of the human realm is that we have all the right conditions for attaining higher "heavenly" states. Earth in its

holiness quietly supports this heaven-human drama and provides everything for our awakening: challenging experiences of mind and body, people to serve, opportunities to practice generosity, teachers to guide us, friends to offer support. Earth is our sacred ship and everything on and of earth helps us on this spiritual voyage. Whether bodhisattvas or angels, sent by God or Buddha, celestial beings wearing gold or gauzy white, the metaphorical images delight our mind and emotions and express a deep mystery that gives poetic meaning to our ordinary lives.

Heaven, the circle, without beginning or end, encompasses the square of Earth; in the center, between the two powers, Human abides in and is supported by this yin-yang principle. The three participants create a mandala of positive and negative space—plant material and the absence of plant material; "form is empty, emptiness is form"; appearances and the absence of appearances.

Supported by the female principle, Mother Earth, or yin, we never lose sight of the male principle, Father Heaven, or yang. The challenge of ikebana is to create a sense of harmony, beauty, and balance between these three elements; the challenge of Buddhist practice is to realize that there is no separation between the three. We as Human symbolize the active principle, Earth represents the inactive, and Heaven the body in which all are contained.

The Seika style depicts Heaven, Earth, and Human in a simple yet elegant and refined way. The three elements, arranged to appear as one, contain no gaps between stems. The Heaven element curves like an archer's bow. Woody branches must be coaxed into a curve either with gentle bending and twisting or light nipping with one's clippers. Ends of stems must be cut at the proper angle so as to fit snuggly against the side of the container, thus preventing turning. A forked bamboo holder or natural branch crook (kubarigi) sits about three-quarters of an inch below the rim of the container to hold the branches in place. A strip of flexible branch material (kaihari) wrapped around the stems and supported by the sides of the container secures the bundle.

Seika is the favored style of Master Noguchi, who created numerous variations from old lichen-encrusted azalea branches for his school's eightieth anniversary show. An ikebana master from Tokyo had come to assist. He sat in a chair surrounded by scotch broom branches, while a female professor of ikebana from Daikaku-ji knelt on the floor beside him, trimmed the excess stems, and handed them over as needed. In Japan, accomplished practitioners with years of experience and professional credentials clean the floors of flower masters' studios, wash the vases, clip the branches, organize the materials, and stay in the background. They are often not included in celebratory dinners, or allowed to participate in major shows. They cannot attend ikebana conferences or teach without permission of the master. The hierarchy within the Japanese flower schools is difficult for Westerners to understand, but seen in the light of training, we surmise that the teacher may be skillfully trying to wear down his student's ego-mind of self-importance. Our Western, individualistic mindset would not accept such training from an ikebana teacher, so we must learn different ways to be honest with ourselves, to be self-reflective and strict in our behavior. We must learn to control and monitor our own childish mind and desires within our sphere of Heaven and Earth. Artistically we must find a balance between mass and space, light and dark, tall and short, smooth and rough, straight and curved. Spiritually we must reconcile with Heaven and Earth, and the middle way of harmonious living.

As I leave the museum, I pass one more time through the "Asian Aesthetics" room to check on my arrangement. The orange lilies, harmoniously supported by Heaven and Earth, look resolute and strong under the overhead lighting. The overall effect is one of calm and balance, attributes that I hope to take with me into the rest of the day.

MORIBANA USING AZALEA, LILY, AND AUCUBA.

The slow day;
Echoes heard
In a corner of Kyoto.

—BUSON

Lessons in a Basket

Early spring is the time of year in central Japan when plum blossoms give way to peach and pear, when the Japanese remember the legend of Lady Izumi from *The Plum Tree by the Eaves*, a Noh play, in which the lady reveals to the traveling monk her true identity as a bodhisattva of song and dance. Lady Izumi's story lends inspiration and romantic reverie to this place in Kyoto where white and pink flower petals anoint the earth and "the soothing voices of Kamo's flowing waters rising among the wooded northern hills... sow in the mind the seed of rebirth in the land of Bliss."

Flowering trees, plum trees especially, were always part of my childhood, not as poetic objects as they are in Japan, but as actual sources of food that my parents grew on their Washington farm. Every year they would fill a cabinet with quarts of plums, pears, peaches, and cherries. "Sauce," they called these jars of canned fruit.

It is difficult for me to find a flower or flowering tree that does not have an image or a memory attached to my mother, or a farm crop that does not have a reference to my father. But on this trip to Japan, my sister and I try to focus on the joy and lightness of the moment without sadness from the past, or fears of the future. Soon enough we will return home to look after our father who, still grief stricken from the loss of our mother, struggles to cope with failing health and his fifth year of kidney dialysis. We don't yet know about the other illness quietly manifesting.

In this spirit of wanting to enjoy being sisters in this wonderful land where we once lived, we stroll through the streets and shops of Arashiyama on a drizzly day in March feeling a little damp, a little cold, but completely enthralled. After a ten-year absence I, like Lady Izumi, "recall those days of yore when, urged by hues and scents, I was passion's slave" and revel in all my memories of Japanese sites, sounds, smells, and loves through the disorientation of jet lag. Arashiyama-Sagano, once a country retreat setting for emperors and empresses, now hosts Zen and Shingon temples, moss gardens, tea houses, a Buddhist nunnery, and the Hut of Fallen Persimmons where the famous haiku poet Basho wrote the *Saga Diary*.

Place names like Dragon Gate Waterfall and Garden of the Lion's Roar add to the poetic mystery of this region which once hosted *renga* parties, where literati, now immortalized in anthologies, drank too much saké and composed linked verse under moonlight.

Even though today more tourists than poets travel the streets and alleyways, forests and farms between the Hozu River and Daikaku-ji Temple, the Arashiyama-Sagano area retains a feeling of ancient artistic ambience. We are transfixed, not only by the moss-covered haiku stones and bamboo groves, but by the folk crafts and art objects imbued with subtle beauty and exquisite craftsmanship that come with historical significance, family lineages, religious symbolism, relationship to the gods.... Nothing in Japan wears a single layer of meaning. The colors, textures, patterns, and aesthetic appeal of Japanese arts and crafts have no rival. Even the Saga School honors this historical locale with the "Scenic Trio of Saga," natural scene arrangements that express the beauty of seasonal changes: "Scene of Teiko" depicts the autumn chrysanthemums of Osawa Pond, the lake in the garden at Daikaku-ji; the "Scene of Takao" shows the autumn splendor of red and yellow maples along the Kiyotaki River gorge of Mount Takao where Kobo Daishi resided for a time; and the third in the trio, "Scene of Arashiyama," represents cherry blossoms and azalea with outstanding rock formations found along the Hozu River. Each scene in the trio is displayed in a low ceramic container with water flowing between groupings of plants and rocks to show pond, gorge, and river respectively.

Caught in the aura of this centuries-old backdrop, we enter a bamboo shop and wander off in different directions. My sister investigates tea ceremony implements, while I find myself in the back of the shop taking in the quiet nature of a medium-sized basket suitable for ikebana.

Dwarfed by larger cousins but standing out in its simplicity, the basket, a tightly woven bamboo one with matte black under-weave and mahogany overtones, and co-joined in a particularly pleasing manner, hooks my mind of attachment, that state of being that initially feels good and fine and harmless, but is nonetheless one of the three roots of suffering (the other two being ignorance and hatred). Dismissive of any teaching that might intrude on my moment of Arashiyama rapture, I find myself thinking, "Can I afford it?" rather than, "How is this plunge into desire 'enslaving' me?"

Hoping that I might lose the "hook" if I leave the shop and distract myself with mere looking, I find my sister and duck out into the rain under the protection of a just-purchased umbrella. An hour later, a little wetter, a little colder, the bamboo basket still maintains a hold over my mind of attachment.

Bamboo is one of the Three Deities of the Floral Kingdom (along with pine and plum); the bamboo forest, a sacred barrier encircling Shinto shrines, protects against evil. Imbued with centuries of legend and poetry, and elevated in Japan to near-mystical status, bamboo, with its sturdy stalks that grow so rapidly you can almost see them move with the naked eye, offers over one thousand uses. Houses are made from bamboo, as are flooring and fences; scoops, spoons, and ladles; bowls, boxes, plates, paper, vases, combs, toys, yarn, musical instruments, weapons.... You can even eat bamboo.

And then there is the famous Tale of the Bamboo Cutter, a basket-maker who finds a magical female child in the stem of a large bamboo. Because her body radiates a celestial light, her adoptive parents name her Shining Princess of the Young Bamboo, or Moonray. She grows up into an uncommonly beautiful young woman that everyone wants to look at and all the men want to possess. But having no intention of marrying and staying imprisoned in earthly life, she rejects all of her suitors, including the emperor; she yearns to go to back to her real home, the glorious moon.

Before I can form a logical reason why I should *not* have this special basket-maker's work of fine art, the seduction of the object and the allure of this temple-laden, Heian-era haiku–haven, bamboo-forested fabulous place overtakes me. After a quick consultation with my sister, I return to the shop, examine the basket, ponder the consequences, and tell the clerk that I'd like to buy it.

I wonder about the person who made this unique basket. Was it a man or a woman? Old or young? How many baskets did he or she make before reaching the skill evident in "this" basket? How many hours did it take the artist to make it? How much of the purchase price did he or she get? As an artist I identify with the meager compensation that most creative people accept as part of their practice, and find yet another reason to buy the basket.

The basket, now carefully wrapped, protected in a box, and tied up in an enormous shopping bag, leaves the shop, Arashiyama, Kyoto, and Japan.

The action of "grasping," as described in Buddhist doctrine, is now complete—I have focused on an object of beauty, desired it, exaggerated its good qualities, wished to possess it, moved to possess it, and now possess it, having been hypnotized by temporary good feelings. In the deluded state of projecting "feel-good" qualities onto an object, we run the danger of wasting our lives pursuing

Figure 1:
Inoribana using gladiola and crocosmia. Original container by Ron Carson.

Figure 2:
Shinshoka using canna.

Figure 3: (left)
Shogonka using huckleberry, leucadendron, solidago, iris leaf, fern, spider chrysanthemum, and aspidistra.

Figure 4: (below)
Sai no Hana using aspidistra, freesia, and hosta.

Figure 5: (left)
Moribana using
azalea and lily.

Figure 6: (below)
Omoibana using
'Stargazer' lily.

Figure 7: (left)
Basket arrangement using nandina, alstroemeria, and hawthorn.

Figure 8: (below)
Moribana using azalea, lily, and aucuba.

Figure 9: (left)
Inoribana using pine,
hydrangea, and ninebark.

Figure 10: (below)
Moribana using bamboo,
leucadendron, and hosta.

Figure 11:
Heika using pine, orchid, and aucuba. Original container by Sandra Dolph.

Figure 12:
Seika in well buckets using aspidistra and lily.

Figure 13:
Morimono using iris leaves
and seed pods, zinnias, squash,
ginger root, peppers, and
walnuts.

Figure 14:
Inoribana using caladium,
tulip, and leucadendron.

Figure 15:
Inoribana using tulip, gerbera daisy, and aralia.

Figure 16:
Inoribana using aspidistra, alstroemeria, and star-of-Bethlehem.

endless material "stuff," or fooling ourselves that we'll never have to part with anything or anyone that we love.

Back in the U.S., I am asked to make an arrangement for the Cherry Blossom Festival. Grateful for the opportunity to transform my object of attachment into an object of giving, I carefully lift its delicate form out of the box, admire its serene beauty, and try to imagine what materials will compliment its pleasant personality. Something light? Tall? Pink? Spring-like? Scouring the neighborhood for plant material, a large apple tree in an empty lot near my building shows promise; a thin layer of lichen adorns each branch and tight dark pink flower buds poke out from under tender new leaves. Apple blossoms symbolize good fortune, so I'm hoping they will serve me well.

Examining the lower reachable branches, I try to discern how each of them will look tilted at an angle under the handle of the basket. With my clippers poised to cut I pause for a moment.... Is this stealing? Stealing is one of the ten non-virtuous actions described in Buddhist doctrine that result in negative karmic repercussions. But hasn't the tree been neglected for years? Isn't it large enough to withstand losing a few small branches? The lot belongs to the city, and therefore owned by us/me the taxpayer. Right?

Seven branches make it into my bucket of water, but not before I remind myself to be careful in justifying taking plant material from property that is not my own. Stealing is stealing. What ethical parameters should protect the Buddhist ikebana artist in America who wants to engage in the Way of Flowers and does not always buy materials from the local florist, as they usually do in Japan? Do we cut the magnolia branch hanging over our neighbor's fence? Trim the unkempt pampas grass in the young couple's parking strip? Help ourselves to the hostas flourishing on the north side of the Baptist church where we're sure no one ever goes? Prune the fuchsia bush poking through the chain-link fence into an empty parking lot? Or take just one mountain laurel branch at the bank building after all the employees have gone home? Temptations all. My own guideline: ask the owner before assuming the branches or flowers won't be missed. And if an owner can't be found? I remember once how my mother, upon seeing neglected peonies at an abandoned farmhouse, helped herself to these prize blossoms rather than watch them die unappreciated.

Before putting the bucket of branches in my car, I shake each one with the hope of leaving crawling or flying sentient beings behind. No matter how diligent, killing, the number-one non-virtuous action in Buddhist teachings, cannot be avoided when working with living plants, nor for that matter in simply living our lives. Walking across the grass to reach the tree probably wiped out at least a half dozen, if not a whole community, of living beings. I vow to avoid all intentional killing and be mindful of accidental killing. As a Buddhist I do not squish the spider that drops out of the apple branch and scurries, disturbed and frightened, across the kitchen counter. I catch the spider in a glass and put it outside on a plant I think it will like—same with the baby snail, no bigger than a mung bean, who rode in on a dahlia.

Agreement among practitioners suggests that we can cut scotch broom growing wild alongside the freeway, or cattails overflowing in the ditches, or salal carpeting the forest floor, as long as our taking doesn't leave a noticeable impact. When all forests, mountains, ditches, prairies, fields, and meadows are owned by someone or something—a group, a government—it is hard to determine what is public and what is private. Long gone are the truly wild unowned places. And more and more, as we move into condos and apartments, we rely on shops, nurseries, florists, and flowers flown in from distant places, not grown or picked or cut with our own hands. Therefore, Kado, the Way of Flowers, must be practiced the best we can by observing the growth patterns and habits of nature wherever we find it. We respect the environment and all creatures that live in the environment, display the buds as well as the withered leaves to show the passage of time, aspire to become as pure and innocent as a flower, and strive for the inner serenity of, say, a white camellia in winter, no matter where or how we get our materials. We humble ourselves by tuning in to the lessons of nature, which show us in a myriad of guises birth, youth, aging, sickness, death, and all the beauty and peril in between.

For the show arrangement I will need one exquisitely shaped branch and one striking flower. Two hours after I return home with my bucket of apple branches, I am still pruning, examining, and testing in an attempt to find "the one." Through concentration and effort, the perfect branch emerges and I work with it for another half hour, testing it with daffodil, columbine, and hyacinth. The lavender hyacinth, so fresh and fragrant in the flower shop, seemed like the quintessentially perfect spring flower, but later, when I insert it into the flower holder, it looks too big and bunchy. It doesn't pass the "*aah*" test, the intuitive recognition that an artistic balance of line, form, color, and texture has been achieved. I take it out and try the columbine. No. Too weak. I take it out and try the daffodil. No. Too yellow. At a nursery five miles from my house I search the aisles for a potted plant with flowers that will be fresh and delicate and... perfect. A pot of pink Persian ranunculus draws my attention. The plant has one mature flower and several opening buds. I can experiment with the mature flower, and by show time the buds will be at their most sublime.

One reference ascribes to this flower "radiant charm," which together with the "good fortune" of apple blossoms feels like an auspicious choice. I take the ranunculus home, cut the mature flower, and place it in the flower holder. Yes! Just right! But now I'm not sure about the branch. It looks too short and too ordinary. It doesn't project forward far enough to create the asymmetrical balance I am looking for. Up until this point only my practices of concentration and moral discipline have been challenged, but now my practice of patience will have to see me through. I'm beginning to question my choices, my skill, my training. I'm getting tired and edgy. I have temporarily lost my spiritual balance and the Way of Flowers.

I search through my bucket of branches to find a better specimen and cannot find what I want. I must go back to the tree. Grabbing my clippers and another bucket of water, I return to the tree, cut three more branches, shake them out, take them home, and examine each one for potential. Finding one that shows the most promise, I prune it, insert it, and put in the pink ranunculus. Perfect! I have another "*aah*" moment.

The basket arrangement, small compared to others at the show, is a quiet, elegant statement that draws attention. At the end of the show, when I return to collect my exhibit, the show coordinator tells me that several people asked about my arrangement. Pride rises to the surface without control. Pride, yet another delusion identified by Buddha, indicates that my ego has reared up in "self" importance to bask in the false notion that "I" am not only real and true and solid but also, well, *great*. Catching the delusion before it manifests full-blown, I muster a quick counterattack of humility.

Once home, the serene basket arrangement maintains its hold on me. I place it on my kitchen counter where I can view it several times a day and savor its peaceful nature. But, like all material phenomena in this world, the flower and branch will soon pass away. Already the ranunculus has lost its full robust look.

By the second morning, the ranunculus's head has drooped forward. Still clinging to the satisfied feeling of a beautiful arrangement, I replace it with a fresh bud from the nursery plant. The apple blossoms begin to fall by the end of the week. After the weekend the leaves begin to dry up. By the following Monday the replacement ranunculus has died.

I keep the branch until all the flowers and leaves have

fallen off. Now, only an artistically pruned stick with lichen remains in the basket. Finally, I give in to impermanence. The arrangement has completely expired and its spirit has long gone. Reluctantly, I take out the branch, cut it up into small pieces to fit into the garbage can, throw out the water, clean the container and stow the basket.

The bamboo basket with apple blossom and ranunculus forces me to consider the passing of time, the fading of beauty, the decay of the body. Despite all attempts to liberate myself from attachment, I feel sadness at the loss of the flowers and the branch. This object of beauty has not delivered on its original promise of happiness.

The futility of resisting natural laws cannot be denied.

The following month, my father found a lump on the side of his throat. In June, one year after the death of his wife, my mother, he had a malignant tumor removed from his lymph gland. By the end of August it returned.

In the crisp sunny glory of late September when maple and sumac begin to bedazzle us with red and gold, and the hills of Arashiyama beckon to thousands of autumn worshippers with promises of the Pure Land, the oncologist delivered a prognosis of "incurable" under the overly bright lights of the examination room.

BASKET ARRANGEMENT USING NANDINA, ALSTROEMERIA, AND HAWTHORN.

Dad asked about a second surgery.

"Too risky," she said. "But we can make you comfortable."

Nobody spoke. We filed out of the exam room and passed through a waiting area with jack-o-lantern banners and fake orange dahlias planted in patio containers. The receptionist, standing on a chair, strained to hang garlands of artificial fall leaves around doors and windows.

The next weekend, my sister enlisted me and my brother to help her can plums from my brother's plum tree the way Mom used to. After Sunday brunch we dug out our parent's old enamel canner from our brother's garage. The metal ring that holds the jars in place had rusted, but we used it anyway. Dad rested in an overstuffed recliner in the living room and gave up his usual after-brunch nap to throw canning tips our way. His eyelids fluttered with sleepiness, but he kept awake to watch the three of us wash the fruit, fill the jars, boil the lids, mix the sugar-water, screw down the lids, and set six quart jars into the canner. Thirty minutes later we had our first batch of canned plums and rejoiced in the clicking sound of lids sealing.

Throughout the last five years, and especially after Dad started kidney dialysis, we had watched our father's body go from tall and strong to bent and weak as he shuffled along behind his walker, slower with each passing day. Now it is October, when the thick stalks of sunflowers once heavy with seeds have been picked clean by crows. Mold creeps up the stems and onto the leaves. Big brown heads fringed with yellow petals droop in the clear fall air. The leaves have turned brown and crunchy. After a summer of following the warmth of the sun, the giant flowers, now spent and unable to endure another season, ready themselves to pass from this world. It is a seemingly cruel inevitability that the stalks will be cut down and discarded.

As Father moves into hospice care and pain management, I take down the Arashiyama basket, put a clump of mauve stonecrop in the bamboo holder, and place it on the bathroom counter in front of a wide mirror. Stonecrop, a sedum that holds water in its fleshy body, seems to live on indefinitely in perpetual hydration. Reflected in the mirror, it appears real and solid and at the same time ephemeral. I'll keep it there until the tiny mauve petals lose all color and begin to shed on the counter; then I'll replace the stonecrop with something seasonally fresh—perhaps pine, or that most heroic of delicate blossoms that endures the adversity of winter... plum.

The camellia flower
Was going to fall,
But it caught in its leaves.

—SHOHA

Flower as Symbol

THE LOTUS

Buried in the rank dark muck of stagnant mosquito-infested swamp water, a brown seed the size of a bean lies waiting; it is destined to give birth to an exquisite bloom that has inspired lovers of flowers and seekers of truth for over four thousand years. This seed, pressed into the rich cow dung silt of tropical and non-tropical ponds has been transported throughout time by riverboat, camel, and elephant, across mountains, deserts, and oceans, from Egypt, India, China, and Japan. Now, the tiny kernel, having popped out of a seedpod like a jewel falling out of a precious brooch, slumbers at the bottom of a pond through winter's dark and awaits the warmth of spring.

As the Year of the Rabbit gives way to the Year of the

Dragon, the seed's smooth hard side cracks open and, like Prince Siddhartha lifted at birth from the side of Queen Mayadevi by the gods Brahma and Indra, a white sun-starved sprout bursts forth from the creamy interior to begin its steady ascent through the heavy mass of worldly life toward the sun of enlightenment.

The Prince, prophesized to be the next Awakened One, ventures out of his protected palace; the seed pushes through the mud toward the surface of the pond. He does not know the way, exactly, or so it appears to ordinary eyes, but follows his life's path to the higher realm above. He looks up and heads toward the high June sun that beats down on the pond to coax, cajole, encourage. The way is difficult and dark, but the sprout, now a shoot, grows closer to fresh air, to the oxygenated life that is its destiny.

The shoot transforms into a stem, pushes up, pushes forward. Nothing will stop it now as it thickens and becomes capable of supporting a glorious bloom five feet above the surface of the scummy pond. The patience, effort, and single-pointed determination have paid off; the flower stalk can stand alone and upright. The sunlight beckons—so close now, within inches, fractions. And then a tight furl of something indescribably precious begins to bulge out from the stem.

On a hot day in August, as the sun rises over the eastern mountains, petals as soft as newborn skin unfurl rapidly. At this moment some say you can hear a sound like a sigh or an "aah"—an audible indication of awakening—before a perfectly formed pale pink blossom with a radiant yellow center triumphantly opens wide to the world. From Ryoan-ji to Hokongoin, the Cloister of the Diamond Law, seekers in Japan move from pond to pond in mid-summer heat to revel in sight and scent. This is *Nelumbo nucifera*, the sacred lotus, the universal symbol of Buddha, the awakened mind emerging from the mud of delusion and cyclic existence.

An ikebana arrangement with lotus flowers reminds us of the promise of enlightenment that each of us carries in our heart. No one is excluded from the potential to become a buddha. All buddhas and bodhisattvas throughout space and time arise from the symbolic lotus.

Lotus tubers, cut into thin slices and sweetened into a delectable appetizer, reveal flower petal shapes in a simple mandala: a representation of the universe itself. The lotus root—which grows best in round containers without sharp angles—as well as the seedpod and dead leaves, can be arranged with flowers on a platform in the Chinese-inspired Bunjinka style. The arrangement suggests the three times of past, present, and future with partly decayed or worm-eaten leaves for the past, a mature blossom or open leaf pad for the present, and a bud or furled leaf for the future.

THREE FRIENDS: PINE, BAMBOO, AND PLUM

Pine, bamboo, and plum—known as the Three Friends of Winter or the Three Deities of the Floral Kingdom—take on deep spiritual significance in Japanese culture and the ikebana arrangement.

Venerable pine, strength of a thousand years, represents Lao Tzu, the Chinese philosopher who, according to Taoist fables, lived for nine hundred years; thus pine represents longevity or eternity. Pine also serves as a reminder of the Kasugayama Primeval Forest in Nara, the site where deities are said to have descended to earth. It is here where Buddha appeared as the Dragon God to the monk Myoe during his time of great yearning, when he desired to immerse himself in the life and landscape of Buddha Shakyamuni. Today, the Primeval Forest in Nara, a World Cultural Heritage Site with 175 varieties of trees, still maintains the ban on hunting and logging first instituted in 841. It is also a sanctuary for dozens of tame deer that roam the sacred forested slopes and temple grounds as symbolic messengers of Buddha's teachings.

INORIBANA USING PINE, HYDRANGEA, AND NINEBARK.

In the Kado Koyasan school of ikebana, an arrangement of two pines emanating from the same branch conveys two forces with a common root or shared purpose; thus the ikebana artist creates the Two Pines arrangement for weddings to represent a couple growing together, sharing a single harmonious life. Pine appears in a similar function as a character in the Noh play *Takasago*. The play reveals the pairing and eternal bonding of two pines that grow "a province apart," one in the mountains and the other at the seashore, implying that their connection transcends time and space. At the end of the play, the Villager tells the Traveling Priest that the pines signify two gods of one spirit who bestow special blessings on poets and wedded couples. The chorus ends with these words:

> A Thousand Autumns bring peace to all,
> Ten Thousand Years makes life long
> while, touched by the wind,
> the Paired Pines sing, inspiring tranquil joy,
> the Paired Pines sing, inspiring tranquil joy.

Bamboo, the most prominent of the Three Friends or Deities, represents Buddha; the rungs of the stem mark the stages of the path to enlightenment. Buddha Shakyamuni loved to teach in bamboo groves, perhaps because bamboo creates a tranquil environment conducive to clarity of mind. Bamboo also captures the essence of the illusory world with its gentle rustling sounds and ever-moving leaves that, when wet, reflect the surrounding world like divine mirrors. Bamboo! Even the spoken word conjures a feeling of mysterious tranquility. Some bamboos live to one hundred years, then flower and die.

On a more mundane level, bamboo represents flexibility, endurance, fertility, and motherly love—the latter due to the parent plant giving all its nourishment to the young shoots once it has reached maturity. When winter gusts blow hard across the land, the bamboo bends back and forth, but does not break. So too our own lives are filled with elemental surges and surprises, sudden changes, shifts in the wind: we lose our job, suffer a stroke, a tree crushes our house—things that can happen to any of us at any time (and indeed, all things that happened to a friend of mine within the course of one week in winter). We endeavor not to break, but to yield, as all storms pass. In the spirit of the honorable bamboo, my friend recovered his health, repaired his house, and found an exciting new job overseas. Less dramatically we might only be required to accept the cancellation of a trip, a missed meal, a late night at work. Do we bend easily and graciously, like the stalk of a bamboo? Do we let go of our attachment to the way we thought life would turn out? Or do we cling and make ourselves unduly miserable?

MORIBANA USING BAMBOO, LEUCADENDRON, AND HOSTA.

During the first six months I lived in Japan, my sister and I shared a large three-bedroom house at the edge of town surrounded by rice farms and bamboo groves. The bamboo, enlivened by wind, shimmered in the sun and rustled under crisp fall skies. Even now, fifteen years later, I can hear the sound of bamboo creaking and the dry leaves brushing against each other under an October sun. I can feel the flexibility of the bamboo as a sensation in my body, a gentle bending that induces calm.

One of my favorite places in Kyoto is the bamboo forest in Arashiyama. The bamboo stalks are formidable in size: as large as an arm, nothing like the skinny stalks that grow in gardens in the Pacific Northwest. A wide path cuts through the forest and leads wanderers to Buddhist temples, Shinto shrines, moss gardens, and tea houses. The slightest breeze causes the bamboo to make their unique sound, a sound that fills your heart with an unnamable ancient feeling akin to yearning and finding all at once—or as the poet Ou-yang Hsiu so aptly described, "Myriad leaves give a thousand sounds—all are lamentations."

Plum, last of the Three Friends, represents Confucius, the Chinese philosopher whose teachings on social order and personal morality influenced both Chinese and Japanese culture. When a plum tree gives forth delicate blooms despite a blanket of fresh wintry snow, we think of over-coming or enduring adversity and view plum as a metaphor for strength when conditions are less than ideal. From the plum tree, we learn to develop our own inner strength and patience when faced with hardship, trials, and painful encounters.

As I watch my father grappling with old age and the dire choice of dying from either a rare form of cancer or renal failure, I think of the solid beauty and heroic nature of the plum tree. He is the stoic plum in the midst of a winter storm. My first inclination is to shield him as I would tender buds against a frigid night, but the tree does not ask to be shielded and the winter winds obey the laws that govern them. The plum blooms through freezing weather until blossoms fall to the ground and make way for tender leaves and fruit.

In a wood block print from the series *One Hundred Aspects of the Moon*, Yoshitoshi depicts the poet Kinto wearing a long black robe and hat and walking solemnly across the snow in the Imperial Palace garden with a spray of plum blossoms lying across his outstretched fan. It is not certain where Kinto is taking these first precious flowers of the year—perhaps he will offer them to Buddha. But observing how Kinto moves trance-like through the whiteness of winter, we feel spiritual reverence not unlike that found in the performance of a religious ritual.

For New Year's Day, a traditional ikebana arrangement would consist solely of seven young pine branches grouped together in a Seika style arrangement and tied with a red or white cord. Bamboo would be arranged on the second day and plum on the third. Today each ikebana school has its own variation of the traditional New Year arrangement. In the Saga School we sometimes combine all three in the *shochikuba*—pine, bamboo, and plum arrangement—and pray to attain the same pure qualities as those of our revered nature symbols.

CAMELLIA

Some say the camellia blossom is a sign of bad luck or ill omen because the spent flower head, rather than dying petal by petal, suddenly drops off the stem intact, akin to a human head under the guillotine. But an ikebana master from Japan sees a more endearing aspect. He points out the protective nature of the two waxy leaves on either side of the bloom and draws a comparison to the love of a mother and father supporting the child. In some instances, a third leaf sticks out over the bud, which furthers the metaphor of parental protection.

Despite my own mother's life-long struggle with depression and my father's uncertain livelihood as a North Dakota wheat farmer, they managed to feed, clothe, and shelter four children with a little left over for school clothes and an occasional movie ticket in town. In their own quiet and inexperienced way, they guarded and protected us until we flowered into adulthood. How humbling when sickness and frailty turned them into children and us into parents as we tried to shelter them from life's storms the way they had sheltered us. But even camellia leaves have their limitations when the flower has exhausted its life span.

In the Japanese tea ceremony, the camellia, with its simple and pure nature, creates an atmosphere of peace and tranquility for the honored guest. The flower does not labor to be serene, but through its quiet unselfconscious nature arises as a role model to be emulated.

In A Flower Does Not Talk, Abbot Zenkei Shibayama says:

> Silently a flower blooms,
> In silence it falls away;
> Yet here now, at this moment, at this place,
> The whole of the flower, the whole of
> The world is blooming.
> This is the talk of the flower, the truth
> Of the blossom;
> The glory of eternal life is fully shining here.

Was this the teaching Buddha Shakyamuni imparted when he silently held up the single flower to his audience of disciples on Vulture Peak?

LILIES

Like the Three Friends of Winter and the sacred lotus, the Asiatic lily can also signify deeper thought and historical lore if we literally look below the surface. To a Kado practitioner, the cluster of lily bulbs that forms around the main bulb after one season of growth represents a collection of "underground" or unseen helping hands working together. At times we need the assistance of many to support our achievements, whether a starring role, successful event, good health, or simply growing up. And even if our fortune should be like the crowning glory of a scented 'Stargazer' lily, we should maintain a buddha's humility by remembering all those who helped us along the way.

In the West, the lily flower represents purity; and the Easter lily symbolizes Mary, the Mother of Christ, who is similar in connotation to the female bodhisattvas of Tara and Kannon. I like to use the lily as the heart principle or element of consciousness in the center of a Shogonka arrangement, the Saga style that depicts the Six Great

Elements of the divine universe. The lily then becomes like the lotus: the buddha seed at our heart.

ORCHID

In the world of ikebana, we sometimes see two bronze boat containers on raised and stylized wooden platforms with prows facing east, an indication that they are sailing out to sea. One boat in the shape of a dragon, the other a phoenix, together symbolize yin and yang, heaven and earth, man and woman. The passengers, two elegant cattleya orchids, sit stoically in the bellies of the legendary creatures. With such royal travelers and the elaborate and mythical vessels of dragon and phoenix—rather than mere bamboo or copper containers—this arrangement suggests something other than traditional fishing boats leaving for the morning catch. Instead, we can imagine dragon and phoenix journeying into spiritual realms, sailing, not on ordinary waters, but the mystical sea of our own inner mind stream, the choppy waters of desires and doubts and endless yearning.

The orchid, one of the *shikunshi* or Four Noble Characters—the other three being chrysanthemum, bamboo, and plum—found in Chinese flower paintings and later adopted by Japanese literati, grows wild and free in the quiet serenity of distant mountains; could it be our own spiritual nature, our buddha seed sailing toward the shore of awakening? Not yet fully aware of its inner beauty and noble birth, this regal flower sits straight and expectant in the belly of the boat, trusting that its fragrant petals will someday unfurl and bloom eternally. We leave the world of materialism and ordinary reality, the world of the delusional dream, and head into the turbulent sea of squalls and storms: our own chaotic world of uncontrolled mind. Fearful, but calmed by our faith, we stay aboard while our helpers, the leaves surrounding us, keep us company, give encouragement, support us in time of need.

In the orchid house at the Volunteer Park Conservatory in Seattle, yellow, white, purple, spotted, and spiderlike orchids tantalize the imagination. The orchid cactus, an orange-red flame-like flower with petals tinged hot rose and stamens bursting forth into six pointed stars, inspire us to believe in celestial realms, in non-ordinary states of mind.

The Flower of Life, a symbolic representation of the divine design of the universe that appears in ancient Japan, Egypt, and India, has an intricate spherical geometric pattern reminiscent of the perfect sequential spiral of a multi-petaled flower. The multiple overlapping circles visually represent the connection we share with all living beings. Certain temple sites in Japan where the

HEIKA USING PINE, ORCHID, AND AUCUBA.
ORIGINAL CONTAINER BY SANDRA DOLPH.

Flower of Life symbols are found are thought to be spiritual gateways or points of "ascension." So too by meditating on the perfect symmetry of, say, a water lily or the spiraling depths of a rose, we enter our own inner sanctuary where worries and troubles recede, and balance returns—where we "ascend," if you will, to a higher state of consciousness.

Through the medium of living flowers we begin to experience the divine, and through the power of symbol we transform flowers and the ikebana arrangement into the poetic language of the heart.

In cold water
Sipping the stars...
Heaven's River.

—ISSA

Sacred Water and Well Buckets

In the early morning hours of an earlier time, a farmer's wife rose before dawn, dressed in the dark, lit an oil lantern, and picked up two wooden water buckets on her way out the door. The buckets had been handcrafted by a neighbor in the village who had made his own tools and selected cedar or cypress cut from the local forest. The wood strips, slotted together rather than nailed, and reinforced with a bamboo rim, produced a tight container that did not leak.

The woman lowered the buckets into the deep well, heard the splash at the bottom, and waited for them to fill. She hoisted the dripping buckets up through the darkness and carried them back to her house, a four-level wooden structure built with pine and chestnut pillars and a thatched roof in the *gasshō-zukuri*, or "praying hands," style. Before starting her daily chores, she placed a small bowl of the pure fresh water on her shrine as an offering to Buddha, prayed to be purified of obstacles and downfalls so that someday she might enter the Pure Land, and finished her morning ritual by making a pot of green tea over a hearth in the center of the floor.

Today, only two or three bucket makers still exist in Japan who create wooden vessels in the traditional style. Like so many other folk arts, this ancient craft has become obsolete, though it is still honored in several ikebana schools.

The well bucket—a near-sacred vessel for transporting water—became immortalized in fifteenth-century Japan by the artist Soami who created the Well Bucket Ikebana Arrangement to please Shogun Yoshimasa Ashikaga, a great patron of the arts and builder of Ginkaku-ji, the Silver Pavilion. Soami's designs took on poetic names: Morning Dew Buckets, The Well Buckets of Moss-Clad Spring, Well Buckets under the Eaves, and Well Buckets of Uji Bridge. The latter refers to an actual event when the famous tea master Sen-no-Rikyu passed over Uji Bridge at the same time Priest Entsu was drawing water. The priest cut the rope to his bucket so he could use it as a pitcher to honor the tea master by offering him a cool drink. An ikebana arrangement with two well buckets and a coiled rope platform represents this historic event.

The rope platform under the yin bucket coils either clockwise or counterclockwise depending on the position of the yang bucket and the source of light where the arrangement will be placed. When well buckets are placed one on top of the other ("piled up well buckets"), the upper bucket symbolizes the yang principle and the lower bucket symbolizes yin. When placed side-by-side, yang is on the right and yin on the left. Materials such as aspidistra leaves, hydrangea, clematis, maple, iris, blueberry bush, balloon flower, lily... are some of the materials commonly seen in well buckets. Materials should be simple and evoke the feeling of summer or early autumn. Pebbles, or a bamboo "raft," can be used to support the buckets and further the suggestion of season and the stories surrounding this traditional arrangement.

Well Bucket arrangements hearken back to earlier times when water rose out of the earth unpolluted and clean enough to drink. When viewed as a metaphor for our own "wellspring" of spirit, the well, a deep, dark foreboding place, can be seen as a kind of circular mandala, or as an abode of the purest spiritual nectar. In this context, drawing water from a well becomes an act of religious ritual—sending down buckets of awareness deep into our subtle mind and drawing up buddha-essence. Recognizing the spiritual implications of drawing water from the ground, we offer the holy liquid to enlightened beings.

SEIKA IN WELL BUCKETS USING ASPIDISTRA AND LILY.

In Buddha Shakyamuni's time people went barefoot or wore sandals; thus a gracious hostess would offer her guest water for washing the feet as well as for drinking. On Buddhist shrines in the Tibetan tradition, at least three of the traditional seven offering bowls presented to Buddha contain water: water for drinking, bathing, and scented water that represents pleasant smells. The other four bowls usually contain flowers, incense, fire/light in the form of a candle, and food—although all seven can contain water as well. At one Buddhist retreat center I know, attendants fill seven cobalt blue bowls with fresh water every morning as an offering to Buddha Shakyamuni. What a refreshing sight! Like deep pools of consecrated elixir.

From every cultural perspective we find references to sacred wells and sacred water rituals involving purification, anointing, healing, and cleansing the spirit. In Hindu mythology humans and all other beings arose out of a primordial sea; the Ganges River that flows through India attracts thousands of pilgrims every year who bathe in its holy waters. Hinduism teaches that River Ganges, named after the goddess Ganga, purifies whatever it touches. The baptism of Jesus Christ in the River Jordan has rendered this body of water sacred for two thousand years. Stories of holy rivers, wells, and springs come from the Chinese, Greeks, Celts, Romans, and modern-day French.

In the Western world of the twenty-first century our culture and lifestyle threaten to systematically remove us from our ancestral knowledge of sacred wells and water, and in turn the sacred stream of our own eternal consciousness. We no longer feel a reverential connection to rain, snow, rivers, and streams. We've lost our feeling for water's symbolic properties of renewal and sustenance. The sacred does not enter into our routine. Water is a utilitarian commodity treated with chemicals by urban municipalities before rendered drinkable; then we buy this precious substance from the city and run it through purifiers to filter out further contaminants. Even though homeowners pay the municipality for the privilege of using water, we waste it by not using it wisely. We run our dishwashers when only half full, and leave leaky faucets unfixed. We take for granted the ability to take a bath or shower whenever we want, for as long as we want. We waste hundreds of gallons of water every day to keep golf courses and lawns picture perfect. And as ikebana practitioners, how often do we heedlessly pour used water from vases and buckets down the drain rather than recycling it by watering potted plants and gardens? Our water habits in the West are excessive and extravagant when compared to developing countries that simply lack enough clean water to drink.

Only when we enter a spiritual sanctuary such as a temple, retreat center, tea room, or church do we see water used for anointing, for ablutions, and for offerings. Yet, in our home, though we cannot draw water, we can still make an offering of water as an act of gratitude for the blessing of pure, fresh sustenance, and thus create positive imprints, or karma, for our future.

In Japan, water for the tea ceremony holds a sense of the sacred even still. In preparing for a traditional *chaji* (celebration with food and tea) in Kyoto, the practitioner must rise before dawn to draw water from a special well between four and five o'clock in the morning. This pure water is then used for making thick green tea, or *koicha*, and for filling the stone basin in the garden. Before entering the tea house the host and guests take a ladle of water from the stone basin to purify their hands and mouth. They do this in silence, thus creating a feeling of peace and serenity for the ritual about to be performed. With sacred water and the tea ceremony in mind, Shingon participants at the Flower Offering Ceremony similarly offer three main items: flowers, *matcha* (a fine, powdered green tea), and *mochi* (rice cakes).

Flowers and water are inseparable. In ikebana, the water level in a vase indicates the season: a full container imparts a feeling of coolness to the heat of summer; a half-empty container helps to allay a feeling of coldness in winter. If we add too much water to a boat container, it appears to be sinking. Very inauspicious! And when we arrange morning glory in a single well bucket we can remember the story of the poetess Chiyojo; entranced by the morning glory that had entwined around the pulley of her well during the night, she ran next door to draw water from her neighbor's well rather than disturb the quiet beauty of the bloom. She honored the twining beauties with the following haiku:

> my well bucket
> taken by the morning glory—
> this borrowed water

During my childhood, Mother grew pale blue morning glories from seed and nurtured them on our sun porch. A memory of her proudly showing me a morning glory bloom—a flower that would fade by afternoon—in a serendipitous moment when mother, daughter, and flower appeared one morning at the same time on the porch remains as a happy imprint in my mind now some fifty years later. My mother, enchanted by the delicate shyness and magical blue quality of morning glories, shared the same delight as the eighteenth-century Chiyojo. Even today, modern-day aficionados at Shingen-ji Temple in Tokyo flock to the Morning Glory Market to partake in the exquisite sight of blooming *asagao* (literally "morning face" flower) still wet with morning dew—dew being symbolic of the transitory nature of all existence.

My sister, caught up in the enthusiasm of these "morning glory stories," recently found two 'Rositas' and two 'Mount Fujis' at a local nursery's two-for-one sale and bought us each a pair. The morning I was finalizing this chapter, I looked out on my patio where I'd placed the two morning glories and beheld an open 'Mount Fuji': one exquisitely shaped purple-blue flower with a white star design radiating forth from a violet-tinged throat. What a joy! Was it a moment like this that a five-year-old girl walked onto a sun porch early one morning and found her mother enjoying the rapture of a newly opened morning glory? I could easily imagine Chiyojo's delight upon finding asagao wrapped around her well bucket rope. Disturbing such a sight would be sacrilegious.

In the fragmented way we live today, the well has been eliminated and the morning glory must grow on an urban patio above the din of jackhammers, saws, and traffic. My water offerings must come from a Brita container I keep in the refrigerator. But we do the best we can to keep a connection with the poetic and the sacred, to honor the gifts of nature and to offer our good fortune back to the power that bestowed it.

Chiyojo understood this union of humans, nature,

and the divine. So too did Yoshitoshi when he created a special wood block print of Chiyojo in his collection *One Hundred Aspects of the Moon*. A distraught young woman stands in the middle of the road looking down on her spilled water bucket that can no longer reflect the moon. The moon reflected in water appears real, but when you to try to find it, you cannot; thus a reflection in water becomes an analogy for the deceptive nature of all appearances, for emptiness. In some of the older traditional designs the Well Bucket arrangement sits on a well filled only with water, which reflects the flower arrangement above.

Chiyojo would have appreciated this reference to emptiness. Later she became a Buddhist nun so that she could be free to write poetry and enjoy nature without the restrictions placed on women of her time. Her sensitivity to plants, flowers, and water imbued her with a reverential feeling for the well bucket, a feeling perhaps we have lost.

In the new Saga Goryu textbook printed in English, the Well Bucket arrangement has been eliminated. Is it any surprise? In today's world of indoor plumbing, we have lost interest in such humble and reverential ideas as sacred water and sacred wells. One more link back to the poetic serenity of a simpler life dissolves.

Luckily some sacred water rituals still do remain. In

Nara, Japan, the Omizutori, or Taking Sacred Water Festival, performed at the end of winter, continues to be celebrated some twelve hundred years from the original event. Eleven priests at Nigatsudo Hall of Todai-ji, chosen to perform the ritual, begin by clearing the site where the water ritual is performed; then they make pilgrimages to shrines and temples, and prepare various items such as paper camellia flower arrangements. Once the ceremony begins the priests are forbidden to speak or leave the temple. On March 1, the "eternal lamp" is lit with a new fire and offered to eleven-headed Kannon, the bodhisattva of compassion. The following day at sunset the priests perform purification rites to pacify obstacles to a successful ceremony. They eat only one meal a day and offer a small portion of their food to birds and animals. Circumambulating the altar, they shake rattles, blow on conch shells, and chant the name of Kannon. On the night of March 12, the priests stand on the high platform of the Nigatsudo and hold ten flaming torches over the heads of the spectators. Sparks fall on the crowd in a symbolic ritual of burning away delusions and the darkness and cold of winter. Spring can now arrive. Around 2:00 A.M. on March 13, the priests draw the first water of spring from a sacred well on the temple grounds and offer it to Kannon.

We might perceive an event such as Taking Sacred

Water as mere cultural entertainment, but we can shift our view and experience Omizutori as a holy rite, a time for all of us to remember and honor water's life-giving properties. More and more we hear of massive droughts and heat waves where wild fires consume thousands of acres of forest land and hundreds of homes; of unparalleled pollution of lakes, streams, and oceans; of contaminants found in fish, whales, and other sea life; of disappearing aquifers and diminishing snow melt. We must remember to honor water.

For the first eight years of my life, when I lived on a farm in rural North Dakota, we pumped water from a well for all of our needs: bathing, drinking, cooking, and cleaning. Unlike the Japanese, we did not directly view our well as sacred, nor did we directly offer water to our Supreme Deity, yet at every meal we blessed the food and water put before us and gave thanks to our Lord for his gifts. Because pumping water and carrying it indoors presented a major task for a family of six, we bathed once a week; and in winter, when the pump froze, we melted snow on a gas stove. Needless to say, when indoor plumbing arrived, we were all delighted, even though this event marked the beginning of taking water for granted.

Still, we had our water rituals. Each time we entered a Catholic church sanctuary we dipped our fingertips into the holy water font—usually an alabaster basin or one made from some other kind of stone—and made the sign of the Cross. In spring, the priest came out to our farm and sprinkled holy water over our fields from a silver implement while reciting a blessing in Latin. We knew the holy importance of water; and as farmers, we understood the life-giving property of a good and timely rain.

Holy water, holy implements—when we follow the thread of meaning from the well bucket, to the well, and to the pure sacredness of water, the Well Bucket Arrangement becomes a link that takes us back to a time when the act of engaging with the divine meant touching, sprinkling, drawing, or offering water; a time when we asked to be blessed or purified. In "Etiquette in the Buddha-Altar Hall"—rules set out by the Shingon monk Myoe in his work the *Mantra of Light*—it says, "During the summer obtain fresh water from the well morning and evening for the water offerings. Do not let your sleeves touch the offering-water bucket." We should view water as a life-giving substance and hold it in the highest esteem, remembering how symbolically it represents the purest essence of "the mother of all life."

Ikebana in the context of water and well buckets is thus a practice of putting the sacred back into creativity, flowers, plants, water, and all of nature. "Sacred," "spiritual," and "holy" are not archaic words relegated to ancient cultures, but words for our new century, for artistic endeavor, spiritual essence, and the experience of connecting with nature. To lose touch with the sacred is to lose touch with the real self, that subtle mind of knowing and being that emerges from great silence and the simple yet profound beauty of a single flower or a bowl of pure water.

Flowers cannot grow or flourish, or live long after being cut, without the nourishment of water. As Kado practitioners, we need to think about and revere, not only plants, but the holiness of water as well. Water is the life of a flower, and of us.

Vajra Flower Bodhisattva

In the very center of the Diamond Mandala of Shingon Buddhism, you will find the Cosmic Buddha Mahavairochana (Dainichi Nyorai, in Japanese) surrounded by four buddhas and thirty-two bodhisattvas. Like flowers in an arrangement, each deity contributes to the whole, but is not separate from it. They offer their unique gift, and in doing so pay homage to the Universal Buddha. Dainichi Nyorai, the Great Illuminator, touches all living beings, and manifests as the individual expression of all the other deities.

Like the bodhisattvas of Song, Dance, Flower Garlands, Joy, Light, Smiles, Bliss, and many others, Vajra Flower Bodhisattva contributes her individual essence to this Attainment-Body Assembly. Limitless are the ways in which her energy works within the field of nature:

flowers, the flower arranger, and the viewer of flowers all partake in the bodhisattva's activity. Individual flowers, as varied as the human heart-minds that perceive them, burst forth from mountains, deserts, and plains like jewels in Indra's net. And just as flowers appear in endless shapes, colors, and sizes, so too ikebana creations, even traditional ones with precise rules and forms, maintain subtle differences. Flowers and plants, trees, vegetables, fruits, roots, and rocks, all the natural materials employed by the ikebana artist, bring forth the essence of the Vajra Flower Bodhisattva's work. She is a spoke in the Great Wheel of human and non-human activity, energy that circulates from sunrise to sunset and equinox to equinox, from the Year of the Golden Boar to the Year of the Rat, from conception to the final breath of life. Vajra Flower Bodhisattva is the healing hand and heart that emanates through living flowers. She can appear in infinite ways to bring flower blessings into our lives: as gardeners, flower lovers, ikebana artists, healers. Nature joins with humans, divine permeates the seemingly ordinary.

One day a friend calls. "How would you like to do a flower activity with two elderly ladies?"

The next week I find myself at an adult family home in the suburbs without any idea of what to expect or what exactly I'll be doing. A friendly face greets me at the front door and introduces me to my new students. To honor their privacy, I'll call them Eleanor and Joy.

Eleanor, a spry and dignified ninety-two-year-old, well dressed and proper with professionally coiffed short gray hair and dainty gold earrings, suffers from dementia. Joy, a cautious yet determined elder who won't tell me her age, wears extra-large flowery shirts with short sleeves, even in winter. She suffers from Parkinson's disease *and* dementia.

At this first meeting, not knowing the protocol, I have neglected to bring flower materials—I'd brought only magazines with great ikebana pictures. But it is a sunny fall day, perfect weather for a walk outside, and the owner of the home has a big yard. Eleanor steadies herself on my arm as we walk down the driveway and around the parking strip looking for plant material. We find dried cone-flowers, stonecrop, and a variety of evergreen bushes—nothing very showy. I detect that Eleanor hasn't yet learned to appreciate the beauty of less colorful textured materials when she points to a wild yellow daisy growing in the lawn and says, "How about that?"

Not wanting to denounce any flower or discourage Eleanor on my first visit, I cut some of the daisies, even though they will soon wilt, and add them to the mix. Back in the house, I invite Joy to join us at the table, but she says she doesn't feel well and sleeps on the couch. Eleanor, on the other hand, looks eager to have a change of routine. We work with the yard materials and do the best we can to create something attractive, but our first arrangement together—an odd collection of dried, wild, and cultivated plant material—lacks focus and a distinct asymmetrical line. Nor is there any one flower that captures the imagination with its unique color or form.

To our next class I bring pink roses, orange gerbera daisies, and an assortment of branches. Joy feels better this time and joins us at the table. Eleanor fetches a green glass vase that she has saved from a bouquet of flowers that someone, now forgotten, had once brought her. Joy doesn't have a vase, but I've brought a small bamboo basket just in case.

I use David viburnum with roses for Eleanor's vase, and the gerberas with Japanese sedge for Joy's basket— both arrangements, in the simple Heika or "thrown in" style, focus on the beauty of a single branch. After placing the flowers to the front with the branches and leaves to one side and something in the back for depth, I take all the materials out and invite them to recreate it, which is the traditional ikebana teaching method.

With furrowed brow, Eleanor concentrates on carefully putting each element back into the vase. She even grabs my clippers when I'm not looking so she can snip off a few extraneous leaves.

Joy slumps in her chair, watching attentively. Her hands shake uncontrollably. I don't know if she is capable of putting the materials into the vase; maybe she will drop them. Not wanting to underestimate her, I hand her a daisy. She reaches toward the gerbera with her right hand, which shakes badly. But when her fingers take hold of the flower stem, her hand steadies. She places the materials into her basket with a sureness that surprises me.

I don't expect Eleanor and Joy to remember ikebana rules and principles, or how to duplicate the arrangements at a later date. Rather, I want them to have fun, to enjoy the beauty of flowers, to soak up the sacred essence of living things with their hands. Vajra Flower Bodhisattva gives us blooms and branches too numerous to count, and the ladies partake in her offering and celebrate the love of living things.

In my short time with "the Ladies"—as I refer to them with my friends—I've learned not to have too many expectations around verbal feedback. And I'm careful about asking too many questions about the past, or about facts they can't remember, yet struggle to recall. But it is difficult to avoid what would otherwise be automatic social jabber—taking a personal interest in someone by asking questions about their life. I want to know about their past: where they've lived, what they've done, who they've l loved; but it's safer and less stressful to stay in the present moment—the heart of any good spiritual practice, I remind myself. And so I try to let the flowers do the talking as we look at pictures offering inspiration for making a *morimono* arrangement, a style often done before Thanksgiving—even though, because of various illnesses, the holiday has passed.

After the Ladies absorb inspiration from the photos, I spread out a plastic cloth on the dining table along with materials, clippers, flower holders, and a black wooden *dai*, a simple platform; then I bring out an array of edible things: pumpkin, squash, eggplant, green and red peppers, bananas, mandarin oranges, crabapples, and nuts. I pray that my years of training will guide me through the rest.

Before piling the fruits and vegetables onto the dai, I go over color, texture, shape, and the yin-yang principle of opposites. On my last visit we had talked about asymmetrical beauty and the importance of empty space, that odd numbers are more pleasing than even. I teach them ikebana principles not because I expect them to remember, but because I want to treat them as I would any other student.

"It's important to have long, round, and square-ish shapes rather than just round," I explain. "Variety is more interesting."

Both of them, still so quiet, listen to my explanation. The grasses I've brought have crinkly dried leaves. "It's okay to use plants with dying leaves," I say, but instead of discussing death and impermanence as I otherwise might, I instead tell them that, "It shows the season changing." Even though I try to temper my talk on impermanence, they look skeptical—didn't I notice that they are old women with afflictions? But when I bring out the pink alstroemeria, Joy says, "Oh, pretty," and Eleanor smiles and looks happier. Impermanence be damned. The beauty of "living" and "pretty" flowers redeems my lesson.

Vegetables, fruits, and nuts do not seem to have the same potent energy as flowers. Eleanor needs coaxing simply to try three crabapples together with one mandarin orange and a few nuts trailing out to one side; and Joy struggles to fill in a gap between the bananas and the squash. Once they create their fruit and vegetable arrangements I move Eleanor's to her room and Joy's to the entry table, since she doesn't have any space on her dresser; then I bring out Eleanor's green glass vase, which always makes her smile; and I ask Joy for the basket. Nobody in the house can find the basket. It has disappeared. Instead we use a rather ordinary pressed glass vase

MORIMONO USING IRIS LEAVES AND SEED PODS, ZINNIAS, SQUASH, GINGER ROOT, PEPPERS, AND WALNUTS.

left over from a florist bouquet. With her eyes on the flowers, Joy doesn't seem to mind using a plain container. Per usual, I make an arrangement in their vases, then take everything out and let them recreate it. Eleanor goes off on her own, putting the nandina branches in at a completely different angle. I'm not sure if she doesn't remember how I placed the branches or if she doesn't like how I placed them, or doesn't care. She seems to have her own ideas about flowers; and since the end result looks good in a Western-style kind of way, I compliment her, adjust the roses slightly, and offer to take it to her room.

Joy puts her flowers in pretty close to how I had them, and says, "You make it look so easy." When I ask her later if she had fun, she gives an enthusiastic, "Yes."

Eleanor has disappeared into her room without a word.

I'm new at teaching ikebana as a healing art, but I'm intrigued by the possibilities that it holds in the lives of those who need the extra joy, simplicity, and beauty that flowers can impart. With the idea of learning what I can about this new twist on flower arranging, or flower as healer, I drop by a cancer center to observe an ikebana teacher conduct a class for cancer survivors.

Her classroom, located on the second floor in a "healing arts studio," adjoins an outdoor space or rooftop "healing garden." This facility has at least three healing gardens: the Earth/Sky Garden, Celebration Garden, and Reflection Garden. Healing gardens are being designed and built all over the world—gardens for hospitals, clinics, prisons, and nursing homes. After decades of alienating ourselves from nature in urban environments, it appears that the world is re-discovering that living plants and flowers provide a feeling of security, comfort, and meditative serenity that are conducive to healing body, mind, and spirit.

Within this professionally designed space, I find a class of about six women gathered around two work tables. Each of the students looks absorbed and content as she concentrates on producing a Moribana-style flower arrangement using various branch materials and roses. The woman to my left looks downright happy. The students quietly practice their new lesson: pruning branches into a pleasing asymmetrical balance. They adjust the flowers to turn up and out toward the viewer as they would grow toward the sun. The teacher comes around to each student and gives an undivided critique. When she's pleased with the design, and the students have made the appropriate changes, they photograph their work in front of a backdrop.

In outward appearance, this class resembles a typical ikebana lesson, except that the teacher is careful not to make the learning process stressful with complicated rules and difficult techniques. I reflect on my recent trip to Japan where I took lessons at our Kyoto headquarters. First we listened to an hour and a half lecture on the teachings contained in the "secret" book, lessons only available to Saga School practitioners at an advanced level. Then we watched the teacher create a Seika arrangement using seven yew branches. She measured the yew with a string—measuring against the container is considered improper and rude—to arrive at the correct lengths for each branch. Using sharp clippers, the teacher cut the seven branches into seven precise lengths and created bundles representing the three elements of Heaven, Earth, and Human. She pruned each branch to eliminate side twigs and extraneous needles, bent the branch representing Heaven into the characteristic Seika shape of curved bow, nipped and bent the top twenty inches or so of Heaven's front support branch in order to create a downward drooping arch—not an easy task, since the yew kept popping upright and resisted the desired arch. Then she placed all seven branches inside the narrow bamboo kubarigi and held them tight with one hand while securing a strip of branch, or kaihari, behind them to keep the branches from slipping. Of course the branches wanted to turn and twist and slip, and so it took a lot of skill and dexterity to hold the branches in place while keeping them secure. Lastly, once the arrangement was complete, the branches had to appear as though they emanated from one main branch—this is the hallmark of the Seika style. If not at first successful, you must keep trying until this look is achieved. I struggled with my own Seika arrangement for nearly two hours. By the end of the day, after writing notes, checking facts with my translator, measuring, cutting, nipping, bending, twisting, placing, and holding, I felt stressed, tired, and grouchy. Not exactly a "healing" experience, and nothing I would ever inflict on the Ladies.

In the "cancer survivors" ikebana class, the teacher told me that the students begin to notice, over the course of several months, how plants grow in nature, what happens when the seasons change, and how change is inevitable. They form a connection with living things, and learn to appreciate color, form, texture, line, and mass. The flowers they take home will be rearranged in a living or dining room, and family members will also gain the benefit from living flowers.

Will Eleanor and Joy be able to connect with nature when most of the time they are shut up in a nursing home environment? Do they notice the seasons changing?

Joy cannot wander outside or engage in normal conversation, but she can interact with the silent language of flowers; and she can answer my questions as long as they pertain to the now, to the immediate moment. "Do you see any that you like?" I ask, as she flips through a book of Heika arrangements.

In an earnest and definitive tone, she says, "Yes, I like them all."

When we connect with nature, something happens inside. Colors look brighter, natural forms appear infinitely varied, a mass of blooms washes over us with its vibrancy. We are comforted by the innocent energy of living things, and begin to absorb the sacred: "Kannon enters into the wild grasses."

Vajra Flower Bodhisattva permeates the flower world. She manifests as flower essence to heal our emotions, as flowers of the field to soothe our spirit, and as herbal flowers to heal our body. In creating ikebana we pay homage to her, and she pays homage to us, providing roses, alstroemeria, daisies... an endless variety of flowers and plants for our benefit.

In normal speech we often say that so-and-so is in my "circle of friends." Isn't this "circle" our very own mandala of living beings? The Ladies at the group home exist in my mandala, and I in theirs. Together we share a connection, a cause-and-effect dynamic as mysterious as life itself.

I know Eleanor loves roses the best, and still recalls a rose garden memory from her distant past, but roses, perhaps because of their exquisite and perfect beauty, do not last long once cut, especially not in the 80-degree heat of the group home. Overriding my fear that she might reject something "lower," and taking practical matters into consideration, I take carnations.

"Pretty," she says, smiling.

With a particular look of peace and serenity that only flowers seem to conjure, she happily contents herself with what I've brought. We turn the chairs around—away from the mammoth television—toward the flowers.

Joy, smiling and eager, pushes her short hunched body up from the couch. Shaking and tentative, she steadies herself against tables and walls, then slumps onto a dining room chair. Her head hangs down but her eyes look up.

Together the Ladies and I will celebrate an hour of flower arranging, as enraptured as children at a magic show. Since I cannot offer them a cure, I offer them flowers.

The world of dew
Is the world of dew.
And yet, and yet...
—ISSA

Inoribana: Prayer Flower

"As we observe plants grow and develop, we are moved with
gratitude for this blessing; our hands are drawn together
unconsciously in a praying position. From within these
symbolic hands, the form for Inoribana was conceived."

From The Essence of Ikebana: Emperor Saga's
Ikebana Art in Kyoto

Sounds of traffic, sirens, and the relentless din of urban
living filter into my room. It is the Monday after Mary's
death and life's sorrows close in on me like a tight, air-
less box.

The elders have been leaving one by one: first my
mother, then my father, and now my ikebana teacher.
Their deaths tug at my mind like a sudden riptide. I say
to myself, "What did you expect from this impermanent

world, this world of dew?" In this moment, I realize how little I'd read or studied about the causes and conditions of human suffering and the inevitability of old age, sickness, and death adequately prepared me for the experience. What could? Still, Buddhist philosophy on the fleeting nature of all phenomena is what I rely on, even though at times it feels like a harsh, matter-of-fact backdrop to my muddle of emotions. Dharma offers understanding and ballast, and hope that the human condition is more than a senseless cosmic mistake. Sangha, the spiritual community, offers love and support. But the power of nature, through its purity, offers a direct connection to the peaceful heart of Buddha. By opening to the ephemeral beauty of flowers, trees, birds, wind, water, and sun, a deep calm emerges. The solace of the natural world promises consolation and a link to the solid place within me that can withstand another loss.

Under the weight of this new passing, the thought of resuming a normal work schedule feels heavy and emotionally impossible. To stay indoors, in the city, feels irreverent.

The Skagit Valley, with its moody skies, great blue herons, and fields of daffodils, irises, and tulips promises deliverance. Maybe a heron will bless the day with its presence. Maybe the clouds will dissolve and the sun will warm the earth—a rarity in Pacific Northwest April.

More reliably, the brilliant tulip fields will prepare my mind for the sorrowful wave I know is coming. Maybe instead of shallow gasps and strained inhalations my breath will return to normal.

I get in the car and head north.

Mary Hiroko Shigaya, my ikebana teacher for eleven years, died on April 21, 2007, after months of chemotherapy failed to deliver her from cancer. A *nisei*, or second-generation Japanese-American, she experienced imprisonment at the Minidoka Internment Camp during World War II, where she met her first ikebana teacher, an Ohara practitioner who taught this ancient Japanese art form with the only materials available: sagebrush and tumble weeds.

Influenced by a high school friend who declared herself Baptist, Mary thought she would adopt Christianity as her religion, but one night in the internment camp she attended a Buddhist service. The teachings resonated with her. Her mother advised that religion wasn't something you could be fickle about; you had to choose a path and follow it. So Mary decided to follow the way of Buddha. After the war, she moved back to Seattle and joined the Betsuin Buddhist Temple.

When I first met Mary she was already seventy, but as youthful and energetic as a thirty-year-old—surely she would live to be one hundred. Month after month, year after year, she offered ikebana lessons twice a week in the classroom of a Japanese retirement home. Patiently she taught all the artistic principles of ikebana I'd grown to associate with her presence: appreciation of line and form, a keen awareness of asymmetrical balance, a tender love for living plants. In Mary's quiet and serene style she corrected and encouraged and nurtured me along until she thought I was ready to strike out on my own— even though I had so much more to learn. I think she knew that our time together was coming to an end.

For eleven years I had the privilege to inquire and prod and delve deeply into what Mary knew so well, what she had incorporated into her own being—the art of ikebana. Mary had a true "flower heart": gracious, self-assured yet humble, kind, generous, and pure. She possessed the attributes of a Kado practitioner: someone who observes nature and incorporates the innocence and purity of flowers into their very being. She was the white trillium deep in the forest, exuding an inner beauty that transcended mundane concerns and the petty chaos of the world.

Through all the years I studied with her not once did she show impatience, irritability, or anger. I suspect she did not complain or whine as I did when struggling to master her art. For over a decade she commented and critiqued, gently pulled out my branches to turn them this way or that, added something here or there, and always, with her sharp eye and years of skill, improved the overall design of my arrangement.

Mary favored the traditional Saga styles, but knew equally well the principles of modern styles such as Inoribana, or Prayer Flower. This style evolved from Shogonka, the arrangement that symbolizes the Rokudai, the Six Great Elements. In Inoribana, the four elements of Earth, Wind, Water, and Fire are eliminated, leaving only Space and Consciousness. The straight, upright, and simple lines of this style, created with no more than three plant materials, came into being at Daikaku-ji around 1990 as an environmental statement for the twenty-first century, a time when even plant material should be conserved. Inoribana arises from the center of an exquisite yet plain container like a graceful pair of folded hands; it is the Zen gassho—the palm-to-palm gesture—of flowers: a prayerful feeling of gratitude, humility, simplicity, and reverence that represents the oneness of Buddha with all beings. Yet words cannot adequately describe the essence of one glorious flower, and maybe we shouldn't try. Mary didn't.

Every Wednesday she greeted me with a sweetheart's smile, asked if I wanted tea, and then fetched it before I could beat her to it. Week after week she made herself available from late afternoon to well past the dinner hour as each student came and went. At the end of the night she packed up flowers and branches and buckets of plant material and insisted that she didn't need any help, even when her bundles grew bigger than her petite five-foot frame. Whenever a student offered to carry her materials to the car she would say in her lilting voice, "Oh, I'm okay." Then—always the last to leave—she'd get behind the wheel and, with that charming innocent smile and a goodbye wave, take off for the long drive home—all this at eighty-one.

Today the tulips will be for her. I want to offer her so much more—a class full of happy students carrying on the school's tradition; an elegant demonstration at the annual Ikebana International show; a completed book on ikebana and Buddhism—but she left too soon, as did my mother, before I could offer either of them the fully ripened fruit of their labor.

As I leave the freeway and head into the heartland of the Skagit Valley, my great blue heron arrives as a blessing at the side of the road. Like an apparition, it stands uncannily still in an irrigation slough as an embodiment of "the wise man," as Native Americans hold. Mentally I bow to its appearance. And the day is sunny. And I find the tulip garden without getting lost. And I feel gratitude for all these wonderful gifts.

INORIBANA USING CALADIUM, TULIP, AND
LEUCADENDRON.

Tulips in purple, yellow, red, pink, white, cream, salmon, orange, and green, planted and tended by many hands, now bloom for the public's delight. I walk among and between them, enthralled and anointed by their energy. The lovely blooms of 'Abra' and 'Angelique', 'Emperor' and 'Empress', 'Miranda' and 'Monet' would have delighted her. All flowers delighted Mary—in much the same way they delighted my mother. Yet even now the two of them, these women of an older generation who would have reveled in this magical display of flower bliss, walk beside me, within me. My mother always planted tulip bulbs in the fall if she could find them on sale, and Mary always used the opportunity of tulip time to teach us how to separate leaves from flower stems and put them back together again in a more pleasing manner. In my imagination I place each tulip into an Inoribana and offer them to the buddha nature embodied in Mary and my mother. These women whose essences have blended into mine and created a new hybrid, who celebrated the flower world with me—one the gardener, the other the artist—remain relegated to memory now, appearances in my karmic dream. I tuck 'Gander's Rhapsody' and 'Golden Duchess', 'Purissima' and 'Sauternes' and 'Garden Party' into all the sorrowful places in this dream. My two invisible and silent companions stroll with me, one on either side.

Admiring the tall trumpet shape of the salmon-colored 'Temple of Beauty', I say, silently, "Look at that one." In rapturous voices I hear them say, "Oh, isn't that something."

Since World War II, when Queen Juliana of Holland sent thousands of tulip bulbs to Ottawa in gratitude for Canada's hospitality during the war, tulips have been a symbol for peace. In Japan, the garden in the Hiroshima Memorial Peace Park displays a stunning array of bright red tulips. With so much good intention for world peace and human transformation, tulips have transcended the mundane and now work their magic on all who can witness their stately beauty. I feel encouraged.

Savoring the day, I linger after all the tulip tourists and their children have gone home, and walk along the river and quiet streets of La Conner, Washington. My solitude is suddenly interrupted by a boy about five walking toward me with his parents. He stops at a pile of rocks dumped in a construction site driveway, picks up one of the rocks, and examines it. His parents immediately command him to hurry up. He tosses the rock back into the pile and trudges after them looking, as anyone would, like someone whose fun has been interrupted. I pass the rock pile and notice how the stones remind me of the rocks we use in natural scene arrangements when depicting mountains and gorges, or marshes, swamps, and seasides. Mary had a collection of rocks and urged me to find my own in order to create the islands of Osawa Pond, the Lake in the Garden at Daikaku-ji. The three islands—Tenjin-jima, Kiku-ga-jima, and Teiko-seki—represent Heaven, Earth, and Human.

Later I will find a forgotten handout from Mary on arranging rocks. The drawings and kanji characters, written by an unknown calligrapher, depict up to eleven rocks with symbolic names such as "prayer rock" and "immoveable rock," along with stones representing the traditional "Heaven, Earth, and Human" elements. An old teacher's manual shows drawings of the rocks arranged in a low suiban container much as you would see stones strategically placed in traditional Zen gravel gardens as points of contemplation, objects on which to rest our mind or stop our thoughts. Rocks in this context represent nature at its most elemental—perhaps what the young boy found so appealing.

Rocks intrigue on many levels. In one Buddhist meditation, we are directed to imagine ourselves as either a piece of wood or a rock. I always choose rock—solid, still, quiet. To be a rock feels right for this time in my life. A rock does not obsess, worry, yearn, grasp, get angry, or have desire; a rock does not have restless inconsolable moods or feelings of sorrow. Beneath all the layers of thought and emotion, I imagine "immoveable rock"— stability, centeredness.

As shops close for the day and the streets grow quiet, I return to my car and head out of town. But with so many thoughts about rocks as symbols spinning in my head, I pull over to the curb to write them down. Inadvertently, I park directly across the street from the rock pile. I decide I must have at least one of the rocks as a token.

What starts as an impulse to take home one miniature mountain rock turns into an obsession to find three perfect rocks: Heaven, Earth, and Human. Recreating Osawa Pond will be a tribute to Mary's lessons on rocks.

I line five potential candidates along the sidewalk and deliberate. Eliminating two, I take the remaining three back to the car where I wash them with left over bottled water from my last trip to the cemetery. (I had placed two bouquets of pink tulips next to my parents tombstone that day.)

The water, warmed by the sun, feels soothing and tender. I bathe the rocks over a storm drain and lay their purified bodies on the floor of my car. With Tenjin-jima, Kiku-ga-jima, and Teiko-seki sanctified, I reluctantly return to the city to face the unavoidable funeral.

The day had been sunny and fairly warm, but now, as we near the Betsuin Buddhist Temple, a cold wind blows up from the waterfront and swirls fallen cherry blossoms onto lawns and hoods of cars. Dressed in our best black outfits, we enter the vestibule and solemnly gather into pews. When the family arrives, the pallbearers remove the casket from the hearse. We stand. A wreath with every flower in every color adorns the top of Mary's casket.

The priest reminds the hundreds of attendees that a person's life cannot be compared to the full flowering of the cherry trees now blooming across the street. "That would be too optimistic," he says. Neither can we say that a human life consists of the brown and spent blossoms now filling the gutters. "That would be too pessimistic." Rather, a human life is said to be the journey of a flower petal falling from the tree to the ground. Some blossoms start higher up on the tree and take longer to fall. Others fall from lower branches. But all petals rejoin the earth.

The throngs of family, friends, students, and colleagues pay their respects to Mary, one by one, by offering incense. In single file we arrive at her casket, bow, place a pinch of ground incense into an urn, bow again, and take our seats. By offering incense we pay homage to Buddha and Dharma and remember that all things are impermanent, as fleeting as the smoke of incense.

Mary was Pure Land Buddhist, and one of the practices of the Pure Land is to recite the *nembutsu*—"Namu Amida Butsu"—an expression of faith and refuge in Amida Buddha. On the back of the funeral program are the lines from a Pure Land Buddhist song:

> When life is fair and sunlight gilds the day
> When fortune smiles and flowers adorn our way;
> Oft let us pause with grateful hearts to say
> *Namu Amida Butsu.*

> E'en though our way leads 'neath a darkened sky
> And to our loved one pain and death draw nigh;
> Our tears may flow, yet trustingly we cry
> *Namu Amida Butsu.*

Two days after Mary's funeral I journey back to the Skagit Valley hoping for a crumb of consolation. Unlike the previous sunny and warm Monday, the weather has turned cold and windy with occasional showers. The tulip season is nearly over. Zipping up my winter jacket and pulling the hood tight around my ears, I head out into the wind and the last five acres of blooming tulips. The swaths of color, and rows of long stemmed tulips, bend this way and that, but do not break. Their resilience in the face of such a strong force seems nothing short of miraculous. At the end of the field, I pause to suck in as much divinity as my lungs can hold before turning back to the field barn. A young mother and her four-year-old daughter, with long hair blowing freely, bravely stagger against the wind. I am struck by the young girl's uncomplaining disposition. Pulling my hood a little tighter around my face, I make my way back over puddles and muddy ruts in the road. Passing a swath of red tulips, I catch movement on the far side of the field. As if on cue, a great blue heron rises up out of the west and flies over the array of yellow, red, pink, and orange tulips: the colorful waves of the Cosmic Buddha's presence. The heron skims across the black field like a promise, like Amida Buddha's vow that anyone who recited his name at the time of death would be immediately reborn in his Pure Land.

Back at the tulip barn, I buy half a dozen orange and yellow 'Temple of Beauty' tulips even though cut tulips are not the best choice for flower arranging, especially the Inoribana arrangement which requires straight lines. Tulips love the sun, that giver of life, and so they twist and turn, arch and bend their necks as they search artificially lit interiors for their heavenly mother. The straight, upright line that recreates two folded hands in prayer will not be achieved for long. But today in the tulip field I imagine a yellow and red 'Anthony's Flame' bursting

INORIBANA USING TULIP, GERBERA DAISY,
AND ARALIA.

forth from its backdrop of aralia and banana leaf. A magenta 'Queen of Marvel' cupped by a perfectly shaped variegated hosta leaf rises above the rim of a delicate celadon. And a fuchsia-tinged 'Garden Party' juts up tall and upright from the center of an imaginary black ceramic container. I envision the tulip with a gently curving aspidistra leaf, their stems joined to create a perfect illusion of one.

Epilogue

Three weeks after Mary died, we had our annual Ikebana International show at the Seattle Asian Art Museum. It was my first ikebana show in twelve years without Mary. She wouldn't be there to greet me with her welcoming smile or give her astute critique of my ikebana arrangement. She wouldn't be setting up, greeting students, assisting us with our arrangements, serving tea and cookies, minding the hostess table, helping with clean up, or doing whatever needed to be done.

Though I was not consciously trying to express my feelings through my ikebana arrangement, nonetheless Mary's presence before, during, and after the show remained. My chosen container, a handmade ceramic vessel with matte bronze glaze and gold interior, struck me later as having the feel of a funeral urn. My free-form

Inoribana, a tall heavenly bamboo nandina with an old pine limb, ti leaf, and one 'Stargazer' lily bud, looked solemn. The lily, meant to be the crowning glory in keeping with the show's theme, "Fragrant Spring," never opened. The tight bud stayed closed throughout the entire show as if it too were grieving. But the green shoot sticking out from the old pine limb held a ray of optimism—a hint of liberation and infinite life.

Namu Amida Butsu.

Acknowledgments

In addition to my mother, Faye Stamm, who imparted her love of plants and flowers, and my ikebana teacher, Mary Hiroko Shigaya, who taught me the artistic elements of arranging flowers, I would like to thank Nobuko Oghi for her continued support of my ikebana practice, and Seifu Noguchi for his inspiration and mastery of Saga ikebana. I would also like to acknowledge Derk Jager for his artistic eye and talents in photographing my ikebana arrangements; Gamo for offering her encouragement and commentary on portions of the text; John Falconer for generously translating portions of the Kado Koyasan textbook; Elizabeth and John Falconer for their inspiring koto and shakuhachi music that sustained me throughout many long hours of writing; and a big thank you to my editors, Josh Bartok and

Laura Cunningham, and the staff at Wisdom Publications for all their insights and hard work.

Most especially I want to thank the many Buddhist teachers in the Zen, Tibetan, Theravada, and Shingon traditions from whom I have received teachings, encouragement and inspiration over the last twenty years.

Gassho to all of you!

INORIBANA USING ASPIDISTRA, ALSTROEMERIA, AND
STAR-OF-BETHLEHEM.

Bibliography

Austin, Robert and Koichiro Ueda. *Bamboo*. Tokyo: Weatherhill, 1970.

Baker, Joan Stanley. *Japanese Art*. London: Thames and Hudson, 1984.

Bess, Nancy Moore. *Bamboo in Japan*. Tokyo: Kodansha International, 2001.

Blyth, R.H. *Haiku—Vol. 1—Eastern Culture*. Tokyo: Hokuseido Press, 4th Printing, 2000.

———. *Haiku—Vol. 2—Spring*. Tokyo: Hokuseido Press, 3rd Printing, 1990.

———. *Haiku—Vol. 3—Summer-Autumn*. Tokyo: Hokuseido Press, 2nd Printing, 1984.

———. *Haiku—Vol. 4—Autumn-Winter*. Tokyo: Hokuseido Press, 4th Printing, 1992.

Brenzel, Kathleen N., editor. *Sunset Western Garden Book*. Sunset Publishing, 7th Printing, 1998.

Carr, Rachel E. *Japanese Floral Art: Symbolism, Cult and Practice*. New York: D. Van Nostrand Company, 1961.

Ferry, Ervin S. *Symbolism in Flower Arrangement*. New York: MacMillan Co., 1958.

Hakeda, Yoshito S. *Kūkai: Major Works*. New York: Columbia University Press, 1972.

Hanh, Thich Nhat. *Living Buddha, Living Christ*. New York: Riverhead Books, 1995.

Juniper, Andrew. *Wabi Sabi: The Japanese Art of Impermanence*. Vermont: Tuttle Publishing, 2003

Nicol, C.W. *Japan: The Cycle of Life*. Tokyo: Kodansha International, 1997.

Nishimura, Eshin. *Unsui: A Diary of Zen Monastic Life*. Honolulu: University of Hawaii Press, 4th Printing, 1990.

Noguchi, Seifu. *My Life With Ikebana*. Translated by Mayumi Goto. Kyoto: Tankosha Topica, 2004.

Richie, Donald and Meredith Weatherby, editors. *The Masters' Book of Ikebana: Background and Principles of Japanese Flower Arranging*. Tokyo: Bijutsu Shuppan-Sha, 1966.

Saga Goryu Ikebana Headquarters (staff). *The Essence of Ikebana: Emperor Saga's Ikebana Art in Kyoto*. Printed in Japan, 2006.

Sanson, G.B. *Japan: A Short Cultural History*. Stanford University Press, 1984.

Shibayama, Zenkei. *A Flower Does Not Talk*. Translated by Sumiko Kudo. Tokyo: Charles E. Tuttle Company, 4th Printing, 1990.

Statler, Oliver. *Japanese Pilgrimage*. New York: William Morrow and Co., 1983.

Stevenson, John. *Yoshitoshi's One Hundred Aspects of the Moon*. Redmond: San Francisco Graphic Society, 1992.

Tsujii, Hoin Koshu. *The Mastery of Japanese Flower Arrangement*. Third Edition. Translated by Bunsho Jugaku and Keiichi Fujii. Kyoto: Mitsuhana & Co., 1962.

Tyler, Royall, editor and translator. *Japanese Nō Dramas*. England: Penquin Books, 1992.

Unno, Mark. *Shingon Refractions: Myoe and the Mantra of Light*. Boston: Wisdom Publications, 2004.

White, Hazel and Zipporah W. Collins, editors. *Roses*. Sunset Publishing, 2003.

Yamasaki, Taikō. *Shingon: Japanese Esoteric Buddhism*. Boston: Shambhala, 1988.

Yao, Xinzhong. *An Introduction to Confucianism*. UK: Cambridge University Press, 2000.

Zeami. *The Flowering Spirit: Classic Teachings on the Art of Nō*. Translated by William Scott Wilson. Tokyo: Kodansha International, 2006.

About the Author

Joan Stamm's interest in Buddhism and ikebana was sparked when she lived in Japan in the early '90s. Upon her return to the States she studied and practiced both Zen and Tibetan Buddhism, and began ikebana classes under the direction of Mary Hiroko Shigaya. After twelve years of ikebana instruction, she received a *shihan*, or certificate to teach, from the Saga School of Ikebana headquartered in Kyoto, Japan.

Joan's first personal essay on ikebana and Buddhism appeared in *Chrysalis Reader* and *Tricycle: The Buddhist Review*; it was subsequently picked up by *Utne Reader* and chosen for *Best Spiritual Writing 2001*.

Joan holds an M.F.A. in writing and literature from Bennington College and a B.A. in art from the Evergreen State College. She currently lives on Orcas Island where she continues her artistic and spiritual practices.

About Wisdom Publications

Wisdom Publications, a nonprofit publisher, is dedicated to making available authentic works relating to Buddhism for the benefit of all. We publish books by ancient and modern masters in all traditions of Buddhism, translations of important texts, and original scholarship. Additionally, we offer books that explore East-West themes unfolding as traditional Buddhism encounters our modern culture in all its aspects. Our titles are published with the appreciation of Buddhism as a living philosophy, and with the special commitment to preserve and transmit important works from Buddhism's many traditions.

To learn more about Wisdom, or to browse books online, visit our website at www.wisdompubs.org.

You may request a copy of our catalog online or by writing to this address:

Wisdom Publications
199 Elm Street
Somerville, Massachusetts 02144 USA
Telephone: 617-776-7416

Fax: 617-776-7841
Email: info@wisdompubs.org
www.wisdompubs.org

The Wisdom Trust

As a nonprofit publisher, Wisdom is dedicated to the publication of Dharma books for the benefit of all sentient beings and dependent upon the kindness and generosity of sponsors in order to do so. If you would like to make a donation to Wisdom, you may do so through our website or our Somerville office. If you would like to help sponsor the publication of a book, please write or email us at the address above.

Thank you.

Wisdom is a nonprofit, charitable 501(c)(3) organization affiliated with the Foundation for the Preservation of the Mahayana Tradition (FPMT).